The

PLEIADIAN
PROMISE

The

PLEIADIAN PROMISE

A Guide to ATTAINING GROUPMIND,
CLAIMING YOUR SACRED HERITAGE,
and ACTIVATING YOUR DESTINY

CHRISTINE DAY
author of *Pleiadian Initiations of Light*

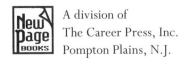
A division of
The Career Press, Inc.
Pompton Plains, N.J.

THE PLEIADIAN PROMISE
EDITED BY JODI BRANDON
TYPESET BY KARA KUMPEL
Printed in the U.S.A.

To order this title, please call toll-free 1-800-CAREER-1 (NJ and Canada: 201-848-0310) to order using VISA or MasterCard, or for further information on books from Career Press.

The Career Press, Inc.
12 Parish Drive
Wayne, NJ 07470
www.careerpress.com

Library of Congress Cataloging-in-Publication Data

CIP Data Available Upon Request.

To all seekers of Truth who are on their path.

ACKNOWLEDGMENTS

My deepest thanks to Alisa Logan, who is the love of my life. I treasure you by my side sharing "heaven on earth" while on this planet together. This completed manuscript would not have been possible without your amazing support and bringing so much to the process of editing this channeled material. Thank you!

My heartfelt thanks to my agent, Laurie Harper, for once again offering your wonderful expertise, support, trust, understanding, and friendship.

My love and appreciation to Reid Kruger of Waterbury Music and Sound for the recording and editing of all the audio material for this book, for the expertise you share with such delight, and for our connection and friendship.

I want to acknowledge my daughter, Lisa Glynn, for being such a magnificent gift in my life, and for the work she has done with the diagrams for this book. I witness you and your journey, my darling girl, with my deepest love and respect for you.

CONTENTS

INTRODUCTION

I was awakened by a brilliant light shining in my eyes. I moved my consciousness toward the light, exploring and touching the essence of the brilliance with my inner senses. I could feel a probing presence, a consciousness within this blinding light opening up through me, holding me as I moved my awareness deeper. This probing energy shifted and began to expand and move, interacting with my consciousness. I would liken it to an energetic echo. I knew I was being called. I could feel the energy of this echo calling me through a unique frequency light sound, and recognized the sound as mine. I opened my awareness into the expanding energy form that was around me, into the essence of a brilliant presence. I suddenly was able to recognize the familiar energetic imprint as my family of light. My Pleiadian family was with me.

Even though my eyes were still closed it was as if I were looking directly into the sun. I knew I was not dreaming. I slowly became aware of a telepathic communion dialogue beginning to open up to me from my Pleiadian family.

The Pleiadians communicate only through a telepathic communion consciousness. One message is transmitted from a collective mind of my family group. Experiencing this telepathic communion is a powerful and overwhelming energetic experience that I still have not gotten used to. The quality of the communion carries a pure and vibrant infinite form of love. The love is in a form unlike anything you normally would associate with love here on this earth plane. Within this unique frequency the love bathes you, engulfing you completely and filling your heart.

This communion experience always brings my heart into an altered state of being, creating a pure focus of the Oneness. It's as though I become my heart and there is nothing else that can exist in that moment. Then it is through my heart that I can telepathically communicate with my Pleiadian family. I become part of the Oneness that is held within the Communion space. I am drawn into the full moment of Sacred Communion with my family of light. This communion moment then dimensionally expands into a timeless experience of reunion, flow, and Truth.

I was fully awake and was transported into the multi-dimensional space that I am a part of, taking in the pure energies of the transmitted message. I merged into the brilliant light as I received all the elements of the message. I AM.

The transmissions I received held the energies of knowledge for this book that holds a profound set of Truths, which are significant for humanity at this time. I could feel the power, the beauty, and the collective truth within this book that was part of my destiny to write.

The frequency contained within this book is unlike anything else I have written. I looked at the energetics to be held within the text and saw how love is embedded throughout. As I opened my consciousness into the beauty held within this weave, the love imprinted through me.

I was shown that the book carries a Truth for all time. I saw that there was clarity within all the sacred energies of this book that will play an essential, timeless role for humankind. I received the full energy of the completed manuscript in one moment. The energy and beauty of the full transmission was overwhelming to me as I took in all the light that is contained within this book.

I became aware that this book is not only essential for us as human beings, but it is a turning point in a new role that is to be established between the human race and the Pleiadians. The information contained in this book will complete an aspect of the Pleiadian mission, the sacred revelations completing a key part of their destiny role on this earth plane.

I was told the book is titled *The Pleiadian Promise* and that it will contain fundamental information that we, as a human race, are ready to receive now, enabling those on the path to be able to move into greater understandings and a new state of awareness of Self.

There will be revelations, essential Truths that have previously been withheld from us. Until now we have been kept in a limited state of being in order to fulfill our human experience of limitation. This is the time for these revelations to be returned to us as part of our natural heritage, enabling us to remember. Now is our time to move forward to new pathways that carry this Truth, re-aligning us to our power.

These revelations are empowering. Many new doorways will be opened as we receive the authorization to move through the veils of illusion. We will be given the self-empowerment to move the veils aside to receive the clear understandings and Truth. This "promise" is what the Pleiadians have contracted to do for us in this lifetime, which this book will reveal and set in motion.

The brilliant light began to fade away from me, and I was left surrounded by a pool of light energy, filled with all the sacred energy from the book. I was holding the love and carrying a deep emotional element of the content of the manuscript. All that was to be written was forged within my consciousness.

The very essence of the book felt woven through my being. My heart held the magic of the moment of revelation, and all of my cells carried the full essence of the material.

I lay still, taking in all of the experiences of that limitless moment of purity and love, in awe of all that I had just witnessed and been a part of.

The next moment the energy of Mother Mary came gently to me. She brought her love and brilliance into me. She carried another message of the importance of me writing this book as part of my mission. She revealed to me in her way that this book will change elements of suffering on the earth plane, and just how the energy of the love and truth contained within this book would anchor onto the planet.

I realized that I needed her energy, her input, into this project. She said she would be with me as I wrote the book. As I now sit writing this, she is here with me, her familiar energy carrying the pure essence of her spirit and love.

A few hours later after the powerful experience with the Pleiadians, my ego mind began to kick in. How was I going to find the time to write this book in my already-busy schedule? Who was going to publish this book? I hadn't heard from my publisher in a few years.

I breathed and let go. I could not and would not explain away my experience. I knew from all of my previous encounters with the Pleiadians that everything would unfold in a timely fashion. The way would be made clear for this book to be written and for the book to be published. I released the need to know how I would achieve this result.

Later that day I looked at my emails. Behold, there was an email from my publisher asking if I was able to write a third book, creating a Pleiadian trilogy! That was the sign that the flow for this book had started. The energetic plane was already holding the full energetic hologram that had been anchored through me for the book to be birthed.

I look back at my very first direct experience with the Pleiadians some 22 years ago. My Pleiadian family first revealed themselves to me while I was walking in nature. I had turned a corner entering an open meadow, and there was their spaceship. The Pleiadians were coming out of the spaceship walking toward me, and at the same time telepathically communicating and opening through to me our sacred connection. They were transmitting and interacting with the aspect of myself that is not human, reminding me of my Pleiadian heritage, of my mission here on this earth plane. It was in that moment when I remembered my full Pleiadian aspect and the mission I came here to fulfill in this lifetime on this earth plane.

This experience of opening to this new aspect of myself was dynamic. The energy that I experienced of my own Pleiadian self flowed into my body, filling my consciousness. I was only aware of the overwhelming love moving through me from this sacred connection. The quality of love was all-consuming. That love held the Truth of who I am, which I could not deny.

That day when I made those sacred reconnections with myself, a forging of my Pleiadian aspect became alive within me. Elements of my own vibrancy anchored through every cell. The quality held within these new elements of myself transformed my whole world as I had previously experienced it. There was nothing that I recognized from before. In that one moment everything changed for me.

I had full memory of my existence before I came into this lifetime. I had full memory of all that I was to achieve here in this lifetime. I had full memory of my Pleiadian existence. An important aspect of my mission was revealed to me: I was to act as a bridge between the Pleiadians and humankind, to bring a new understanding to humanity of who the Pleiadians are and what they bring to support us in this transitional phase on the earth plane. They bring the teachings of Truth to humanity, to move us out of the illusion so that we can make our way back into a personal connection to our Higher Self.

The entire experience was shocking to my human part. There was definitely no going back to who I had been prior to this experience. This was a life-changing event, creating a huge turning point over which I had no control. My ego mind was reeling, trying to understand and take in what had just taken place. My human mind grappled mightily with the full experience. The experience was too strong for me to deny, and yet I didn't want it to be true. I was thrown into a lot of turmoil.

My whole energetic body transformed at that time. I was carrying the fully activated energy of my Pleiadian self, and it took many months before I fully integrated that powerful light aspect into my physical form. My Pleiadian family stayed close by my side as I went through a complete metamorphosis.

This integration process took time and I finally came to an understanding of my own transformational process. I was shown the truth of myself as a human being—that I have come here to have a human experience in this lifetime, and at the same time to open to my full Pleiadian aspect. My Pleiadian aspect is here to support the completion of my mission and to support the unfolding of my human aspect.

I came to a Truth that gave me clarity and acceptance of my awakening. Only the Oneness exists. Pleiadians, humans—we are all part of the God Consciousness. I exist *and* I am part of that Oneness. There is nothing else but this Truth. From this place of understanding I was able to let go and move forward on this new path of living consciously side by side with the Pleiadians. I was able to fully accept my process. My journey with the Pleiadians has continued to unfold and has been a powerful catalyst for transformation within me over the last two decades.

For my 60th birthday I was given guidance to retrace my steps back to where I had my first awakening by the Pleiadians. I knew this would be a life-changing event. I was returning to a sacred place for me: the place that was a turning point in my life. I was told that by returning to that energetic experience I would be repositioned on a new path within my connections to the Pleiadians. I would retrieve energies now that I was unable to process and receive at that earlier time so many years ago.

As I arrived at my sacred place I was shaking. I walked and merged into the deep essence of experience, re-entering the moment that was being held for me within this holy place of remembering and reconnection to my heritage. The meadow was vibrating light consciousness, the space filled with the Pleiadian ship. I was moved, merging with my Pleiadian family. I was embraced, celebrated for all that I had completed with them on this earth plane up to this point in time. Simultaneously, I was presented with the multidimensional elements of my Pleiadian potential and potency, aligning me to my full place within the Galactic Community. I was shaken with the sheer force of my light! I consciously *let go*, opening up to receive all that had been waiting for me.

I know that I have gone through my next step of metamorphosis. I am just being with each moment-to-moment experience, opening up to my many multidimensional levels within. I am grateful and filled with awe at my journey.

I am spending my time bringing the Pleiadian initiations out to the world and supporting people in making their unique connections to the Pleiadians. I transmit messages of truth and understanding of this transitional time of our earth plane, and enable individuals to reclaim and reconnect to their personal power.

I share with you my experience of witnessing the infinite deep love and commitment that the Pleiadians have for us as a human race, how they honor our free will and at the same time encourage us to give them permission to support us. We are not alone. They speak of the importance of us having our full human experience while we move back into our Spiritual aspect. They offer initiation tools to build and develop our spiritual connection to ourselves. They offer simple truths to enable each one of us to move forward, individually and collectively, and at the same time they honor our own individual timing. They offer a continual outpouring of love and support, a hand extended out to each one of us, as we move forward on our unique paths here on the planet.

After finishing my second book I was driving back from being in a cabin out in the wilderness. I had just spent 10 days writing the book and had spent most of that time in direct contact with the Pleiadians to bring in the strong initiations to be anchored in the book. I was tired but satisfied that I had been able to fully translate these energies to the manuscript.

My partner was driving and we were on the Gunflint Trail in Minnesota, heading into Grand Marais for a much-needed break. Suddenly the Pleiadians said, "Now we will take you to your new home." We were directed to turn this way and that, and there on the side of the road was a "for sale" sign. We turned into the driveway and went down a winding track to a large house. We got out of the car and stood on the property. We immediately knew that this was our land. The emotion was strong. There was a compelling energy that this was our place and that the land had been waiting for us to come. An unknown force was receiving us, and yet the energy felt familiar. We could feel an undeniable pull within our hearts; we were home. This was where the Pleiadians wanted us to live to begin the next phase of "the mission."

We walked to the side of the house and looked down. Below us was an incredible beach. The shoreline stretched around in a giant arc. There was an open meadow below us and we could feel the immensity of the space and the strong force of Lake Superior greeting us.

The very next day we arranged to see the property and house with the selling agent. The house was a mess. Actually, the house was almost unlivable by anyone's standards. There was a powerful force of energy emanating from the land surrounding the house. The land included that amazing beach below. The call from that unseen force was compelling and we knew no matter what we had to answer that call.

We looked at each other, shaking our heads, and then we asked each other, "Are we going to allow this adventure?" We said yes. We were both reeling. This project seemed like an almost impossible task, to move into a broken-down house out in the middle of nowhere.

Still we put in an offer on the house, and two days later the offer was accepted. The house was ours. Our adventure began.

The Pleiadians wanted us to move in immediately. This was where we needed to be. It was the middle of winter with freezing conditions in a house that had an ineffective heating system and structural design. You could literally see the wind blowing up the carpets in some areas of the house. The roof was falling apart and we had ice lining the inside of the windows. We had to let go and trust our experience, knowing that we were being held, and most importantly we knew we were in the right place.

The Pleiadians shared with us that we needed to be in this pristine wilderness space to accomplish the goal. We were told that we would be building a series of Communication Portals so that we could interact with the Pleiadian and Galactic Community in an unparalleled, clear communication space. They told us we would go through a powerful transformational process during this journey of constructing the Communication Portals.

The Pleiadians gave me very specific directions. We were to construct three individual Communication Portals that would form an energetic receiving station for the re-entry of the Galactic Community. They shared that this receiving station would be a main artery on the planet for re-entry and that the Communication Portals themselves would carry a pure multidimensional space. It would enable the Universal Community to communicate through to us in a higher dimensional frequency and the Portals would anchor the new frequencies in place for the planet. They told me that it would take a number of years until it would be fully operational.

When my partner and I moved in, Grand Marais was still deep in winter with a lot of snow and freezing temperatures. It would take some months yet before we could layer the first dimensional levels for the beginning of the first Communication Portal.

We found ourselves being held in a pure expanded space in the house and on the land. We were taken off planet daily to move through a strong initiation process with the Pleiadians, and we became aware of Beings from the Galactic Community around us as well. We were moved through a series of initiation processes to align us energetically to the land and to prepare us to play our role in building and activating the first Communication Portal in the spring. Some days we were unable to move because of the powerful energies anchoring through us. The dimensional energies were extreme. Yet there was a deep peace within me, a feeling of rightness to be taking these new steps forward. There was a feeling of an unlimited expression of myself being fully realized in this pure space, and a feeling of deep gratitude and appreciation for all that I had been given. It was as if our world, as we had known it, was gone. We were in a constant state of not knowing who or where we were. We went through a huge readjustment period for months. Gradually we began to feel like we were coming home, as we merged and became one with the energy of the land. We knew this initiation was necessary to be able to play our full roles in anchoring the openings of the Portals.

We kept letting go, surrendering. My partner and I often looked at each other and asked, "How did we get here?" And we reminded each other often, "We said yes to this adventure."

As the weather warmed up and the snow melted we were finally able to step onto our beach for the first time. It was a sacred moment, a pure experience of being fully received, of coming home.

We were deeply moved as we were received by the Pleiadians and acknowledged by the Galactic Community for this crucial step of returning, to have been willing to return and take on this sacred role. We were acknowledged as part of the Galactic Community, playing our part in this collective mission.

This was a humbling and glorious homecoming experience for me. I knew in that moment that whatever happened, this move was all worthwhile. Everything was in hand. I knew we would have everything we needed to complete that which needed to be completed, and it would all happen at the perfect time.

There are strong natural forces on the land, and the energy of the spirit of Lake Superior's vastness is beyond description. Our land was to play an influential role, as it became an activated central Receiving Station for the planet.

We did a shamanic ceremony and bonded strongly with the natural forces on the land. We had fires on our beach as we watched the sunrise in the early morning. We were filled up with energy from these experiences. It was like being fed and deeply nourished after being without food for a long, long time.

Once the snow melted I received specific directions from the Pleiadians to begin to open the first Communication Portal. They showed me that there were eleven different dimensional layers to be activated individually before the Communication Portal was going to be fully operational.

As we began preparing the crystals and stones for the activation of the Portal, I sensed a powerful force within the Lake beginning to respond. There was a transmission of light that began emerging from under the water. I could feel it rising upward to align with the crystals and stones as they were being programmed in readiness to be placed. This was the first dimensional layer to activate the Communication Portal.

There was an enormous outpouring of light as the dimensional settings in the Portal began to fully activate on our land. We found ourselves surrounded by the Pleiadians and Beings from the Galactic Community. Each had their own unique roles to perform, and they came forth to play their parts in the activation of this first multidimensional opening of the Portal.

Simultaneous to the opening of the Communication Portal, we became aware of an outpouring of light beginning to open in the form of a light Portal out in the water. We could see an outline lit up on the surface of Lake Superior. This energy of the Portal aligned directly through and into the Communication Portal. We experienced the powerful presence of the Lemurians coming and taking their place, merging with us all as the Communication Portal went through a further expansion and anchoring.

When the first energetic light waves were set in motion, there was an explosion that expanded light rays throughout the property, and they began to connect to the Portal in the water.

This experience was truly otherworldly and amazing to be playing our part and merging with so many Beings. In that moment of telepathic communion, within the Oneness, we experienced a powerful reconnection being forged with the Galactic beings and the Lemurians. As we laid each dimensional level of the light waves in that Communication Portal we went through continual, unfolding dimensional transformations.

The Pleiadian ships were always present supporting us in this intense physical energetic birthing process within our cells. Each layer of energy that we built within the Portal created a magnetic light force that kept us awake most nights. Between 3 a.m. and 4 a.m., the Portal would call us and we would go under the night sky into the Portal. From the Portal we would always have to go onto our beach to light a fire and to watch the sunrise. As we stood before the fire waiting for the sun to rise, I could feel a powerful integration take place through me. I received the strong Christ energy held within the sun even before it began to birth over the horizon.

At those moments it was so easy to feel the total support from so many realms at the same time, enabling me just to let go and Be more and more.

There was the continuing process of experiencing the sacred connections with the Pleiadians, the Galactic beings, and the Lemurians as more layers of the Communication Portal were activated. I could feel this magic birthing within me and I could experience my own untapped power merging with all the forces of the Universe.

I was in awe of the birthing of the unlimited force of my pure natural power that was rising through me. I witnessed myself in my multidimensionality. I was in the middle of my sacred journey being birthed moment by moment.

Every day we witnessed the full energies opening in the Lemurian Portal out from the house in Lake Superior. We frequently saw the Pleiadian ships directly above the Portal creating strong transmissions of energy that further aligned the energies of the Communication Portal.

We began to regularly experience the Lemurians present with us. They were not only supporting us in our transmissions within the Communication Portal, they would also often come onto our beach, joining us at sunrise. There were Lemurian Beings on the rocks witnessing us, and they brought with them a commanding yet soft frequency of light that supported our integration. Their energy carried a quality of beauty that was uplifting and sacred.

This entire process was life changing and incredibly powerful and, yes, often unsettling at the same time. We were continually going through intense energetic re-adjustment that brought us into a new multidimensional setting within our bodies. We were being aligned to this new multidimensional flow that was opening up through our land. It seemed like there were no boundaries between our physical bodies and the birthing energies of the Portal.

Words cannot accurately describe these profound experiences of which we continue to be a part. I can only say that I am continually held in a state of grace. At some moment, we would re-emerge into the business of the third dimensional world, to face the many details of life, and have our human experience. This unfolding process of completing and activating all 11 dimensional layers of the first Communication Portal took us nearly 15 months to complete.

I awoke one morning and could feel a recalibration taking place within my cells. I knew immediately that I was being prepared for the next phase of our mission, activating the second Communication Portal. I could feel an intense communion with the Pleiadians, Galactic Beings, and Lemurian energies working with me. This change in my energy was essential to allowing me to be able to fully align with the forceful new recalibrations that I knew would be taking place on our land. With the upcoming activation of our next Communication Portal there were going to be significant dimensional changes taking place.

We began the preparations. I was excited and filled with a deep satisfaction and joy about the upcoming activation. I knew this was going to play a significant role on the planet at this time. This next step would be to open another element of the Receiving Station that the Pleiadians, Lemurians, and the Galactic Council had spoken to me about. I knew that we were going to be activating an extremely vital aspect of a main branch of energy for the planet. In retrospect I was right.

The activation of the first levels of this Communication Portal created a huge movement dimensionally. This process began on our land and moved outward with a force of light across the planet. It flowed into the multidimensional realms of the Universe and deepened the alignment to the God Consciousness grid.

In that moment there was a huge shift of consciousness anchored onto the planet, a lifting of veils that had kept the pure truth of light away from our awareness. The energy of the "new dawning era" expanded across the planet. There is an expression—*the wheel turns*—that really applies to this movement, taking us to a new consciousness of empowerment for humanity.

After activating the second Communication Portal I found myself alone on the land for 10 days. I had no plans and was looking forward to some quiet, reflective time to myself.

Day one I was taken off planet. Nine days later I was returned to the house in a completely transformed state. I did not recognize myself, nothing was familiar, and this was a new beginning.

I was merged into the Higher Realm settings of myself for deep initiations. In this pure space I was aligned to a higher authority of my Self. I was initiated to work with the Higher Realm gifts, enabling me to work out in the world carrying a higher authority for transformation with individuals and groups that would bring profound change.

This off-planet experience brought me to yet another transformational step within myself. I became aware of another essential aspect of my mission on another level, and my commitment was held in a different space of energy. My understanding of my role here was complete. No more questions, no more wondering. Just being.

I found myself in a complete state of freedom from my human aspect, no interference from the third-dimensional ego mind. Through this deep process of re-alignment, a new level of communication lines was birthed through me. This process filtered through a clear and concise light form of energy, enabling me to bring forth higher levels of teachings for all to receive.

The Pleiadians began to work much more meticulously with me. This enhanced flow brought me into another state of being within the other dimensional realms. This allowed me to align and understand the process and sacred design held within the Universal Community from another dimensional perspective.

My relationship and awareness was transformed with the Galactic Community, the Galactic Council, the Lemurians, and the Spiritual Realms. I have come to understand that they are all working collectively, playing their parts, for the complete transition of humanity on our earth plane. Each group is assuming a specific role within the one collective group mind, as part of the Universal team.

Each one of us has a unique role to play and now is our time to step forward in a new way. The information and initiations within this book are designed to move us into our changing role so that we can take our place on this Higher Realm level to complete our mission.

The energy on our land in Grand Marais has been and continues to be extreme. There has been a total transformation within both Communication Portals. The energies from the Portals are transmitting this new dimensional frequency throughout the planet and are aligning to the Crop Circles, creating a Sacred Matrix. This Matrix carries the agreement of this time, and it holds the Sacred Texts that we all carry within us as the dimensional openings occur. This collective energy carries all that we need for our state of awakening. The energy between the Communication Portals and the Lemurian Portal forms a pyramid structure of light, and I am aware of the perfect synergy being held within this pyramid structure.

The Pleiadians have shown me how to move myself even further away from the illusion so I can focus differently within moments to create and birth this new weave of light within my life. The Communication Portal's role is assisting with the stabilization of the energies on the planet, as well as supporting us during this energetic phase of transition that is here for each one of us.

There are still many more activations within the Communication Portals to take place. They will only become fully operational when we are ready to navigate and utilize the pure forms of consciousness that will be present on the planet by this activation.

As the third Communication Portal becomes fully realized, it will play a determining role in the completion energy of the first and second Portals, resulting in the birthing of the completed Receiving Station here on our land.

This is the mission to which I have said yes. This is all I need to know right now. This journey continues to unfold me step-by-step, moment-by-moment.

I want to welcome those of you who are about to read this book. I want to acknowledge you as you embark on another step in your sacred journey. I feel an enormous gratitude to play my role in writing this book, and I am in awe of the multitude of higher beings sharing this path with me. I continue to birth and expand, becoming a multidimensional conduit for this sacred purpose.

My love and blessings to all of you Seekers,

Christine Day

Introduction From the Pleiadians

Beloved ones, we greet you.

Our role at this time is to bring the activation of "the Promise" energy to you on planet Earth. This Promise energy initiates an important completion phase of our mission and enables you to move forward to complete your mission. One aspect of the Promise energy is designed to transmit initiations that will remove a series of veils, seals, and filters that have been placed within your physical structure, which has limited your access to your Higher Realm consciousness. These implants have been limiting your experience for many lifetimes to allow you to have a full human experience. We will talk more about this later.

We bring you Knowledge, a series of Truths to support you as you navigate your way to returning Home. For lifetimes we have been on the earth plane assisting you in the different phases of your awakening. Now you are reaching a completion phase in this "new dawning" era. We move into a final phase of assisting you, by activating the Promise energy as our gift to all humanity. This is our gift to the entire Collective God

Consciousness, and this gift was pre-ordained, written within the destiny of planet Earth.

We are here with you in this moment of time to bring forth information for you to access, bringing the revelations that are yours to receive now, as part of your collective birthright. This is the time for your sacred passage to the next phase of your journey, returning Home.

There is a timeless space that exists beyond the limited third-dimensional realm of illusion, where all possibilities exist for you to rejoin your Self. This limitless space of time holds the multidimensional form of your consciousness, where your full existence resides. You are ready for this to be revealed to you; you are ready to return to this meeting place.

"You are who you have been waiting for."

This is a notice going out to all who are ready to step forward and begin this exciting next phase of your experience here on planet Earth. This is a different time, like no other in the history of the Universe. Within all the collective energetic moments that have ever been, there never has been a moment like this.

This is a multidimensional moment that has been opened up at this time. We liken it to a doorway of newness that gives you the choice to transition beyond the illusion that has held you for lifetimes. With the Promise energy, an opening is being held for you to move beyond all third-dimensional illusionary experiences, allowing you to move forward into the natural expression of your ability to be independently you within a multidimensional level.

Feeling limited and insignificant has been a strongly anchored aspect of the illusion that exists on your earth plane. You have been waiting to be saved, to be shown how, to be given the information, and to be given the understanding. Now you will be given back your own knowledge and sacred insight. This is an energetic aspect of the Promise that we have made to you. You can move into a self-realization process as you release the implants that have kept you in a separated state from Truth, enabling you to receive these powerful initiations within.

We honor your process so far and witness that which is deeply rooted within you from your third-dimensional experience on this earth plane. We honor your human aspect and the unfolding of your own storylines that you have lived and experienced. We know and are aware of your readiness to now engage with this full spiritual aspect of Self.

Your spiritual aspect has been lying largely dormant on the other side of the dimensional veils, beyond your third-dimensional experience. There has been a process set in place that has been woven into a part of the full design to keep you separated from your spiritual aspect. Veils have been set in place to keep you rooted in this state of illusion. These have created a limitation of your ability to perceive Truth and to be able to stabilize and retain those Higher Realm connections to Self.

A big part of the grand design was to block your ability to perceive your spiritual aspect. This was achieved through placing a series of seals and filters within your physical body to maintain this separated state. These seals and filters are implants that were designed to activate energetically at birth. You came onto this planet with these implants in place to hold you to in this limited state of illusion. They have played a successful role keeping you separated from your spiritual higher consciousness, keeping you in a separated space from being able to experience the truth of your unlimited potential and your sacred connection to the God Consciousness state of Oneness.

Many of you have been given inaccurate information about these implants within you. Some of you have drawn the wrong conclusions about them. Some of you feel as though the implants have been placed in order to control you, that you are a victim of them. This is not the truth. You are not a victim and never have been a victim. It is important that you open to the full understanding of the truth that you pre-agreed to have these implants in order for you to have your full experience of separation on the earth plane.

These implants have allowed you to have the full spectrum of the illusion that is played out here within the human drama. This is why you came to planet Earth: to have a human experience in this illusion. You have agreed to have this experience. Your human aspect has allowed you to be totally immersed in the emotional drama that exists on this planet. So it is important for you to claim your experience and know that this is what you pre-agreed to be a part of. You said yes. You have been fully engaged in the playing out of your human drama. You have had the direct experience of being locked into the illusion of your insignificance and powerlessness.

Gradually, over many lifetimes, you have evolved and have reached out to find something more of yourself through your own evolution. This has been the sacred design of your personal mission and journey, and you have had the experience of waking up to other aspects of Self. Within this unfolding, a large part of you has remained behind the veil. You have been limited in being able to stabilize and anchor within the many direct spiritual experiences you have encountered with your Higher Self.

In the larger picture within the Universe that exists beyond this third-dimensional illusion, know that this whole experience, over all lifetimes has taken place in "a moment of time," like the blink of an eye. You have been extremely limited by the illusion of time that has been anchored on the planet. So while all your experiences have seemed interminable, in reality they have been but a moment.

In past lifetimes you have ended your incarnation, left your physical body behind, and moved onto the Higher Realms and back into the full alignment of Truth. Your Blueprint for this lifetime is completely altered, and is vastly different than any other lifetime lived. You are moving into this next phase of evolution while still in your physical body, being birthed through a sacred imprint design, and aligned back to Truth of Self.

The removal of these implants will enable you to step forward and experience the Universal Community in full consciousness within the Oneness. This will allow you to begin the next phase of your mission on the earth plane by fully taking your place. It will allow a deep fulfillment within, as you are able to move into a completion of your mission here. You will be able to work consciously from your multidimensional perspective while still being within your physical body.

Know that it is you who will move beyond the veils at this time through your own self-resurrection process. You will initiate your own reconnections by going beyond illusion because you will have the natural resources and tools within you to do so. The removal of the seals and filters will unveil the clarity and Truth to you, revealing your true state of Being.

This is the time. It is just that simple. You have completed this key phase of your experience in this limited form within the illusion and now you move on. There is nothing complicated about this, nothing to deeply understand about you within this next step of your process.

We will play our role with the series of energetic transfers that are involved within your unfolding, holding a space for each one of you as you begin this transformation of your state of being on the earth plane. With your sacred Self fully realized on this new dimensional setting, we will be able to interact with you on a much more personal level. Our relationship with you will transform, for it will be deeply embedded through our joining fully with you within the Collective Consciousness of the Oneness where we can naturally commune.

Now is the time to reconnect to your place beyond the veils, to re-align your consciousness to the energetic form of Self. As you transform through the removal of these implants, you will easily gravitate toward your sacred reconnections. All these sacred reconnections are held in a pure network of light. Your Blueprint of Light consciousness exists within a framework of multidimensionality. We liken this energetic form to a huge womb that carries a powerful network of consciousness light. This womb is infinite and fluid. This is a network made from pure light consciousness. This is an aspect of the Collective God Consciousness. The purpose of this womb is to hold the full Blueprint of your timeless Self, enabling you to align to your multidimensional purpose and greatness.

This space has its own creation energy, enabling you to emerge and create your own rebirth through its Blueprint network of light. This is your time to enter the pathway that moves you through your sacred birth canal so that you can re-emerge back into this sacred aspect of you.

This phase of your journey involves you waking up to realign to your full spiritual nature, while at the same time keeping this physical form of your body. As you align to this full aspect of Self, you will begin to naturally anchor the aspects of your Blueprint light into the cells of your body. This energy is electrical in nature and will activate a complete shift through you, transforming all of your cells and systems within your physical body.

As you move into the full alignment to your Blueprint light there will be an activation that strongly ignites a rejuvenation process through your full physical systems. This Blueprint frequency merges into your energetic field, mirroring the high-frequency pulses that your Blueprint transmits.

Yes, there are going to be deep recalibrations taking place within your physical body as you go through this powerful electrical change within all of your systems. Your energetic body will also go through a metamorphic change. You will begin reopening centers in your brain that you have not been able to access up to this time. As your systems are electrically changed you begin a natural expansion, utilizing more of your unlimited capacity.

Your telepathic abilities will open. The central power centers within your brain will become operational for the first time. These centers hold the settings that allow you to travel beyond the veils and be able to self-realize, to recognize your divine aspect of Self.

There will be a deep adjustment period for you to work through on both the energetic and physical levels of your body. You will initially have a challenging learning curve in navigating from the Higher Realm setting and being able to operate effectively on this earth plane in your day-to-day life. Your senses will be heightened through the adjustments from your Higher Realm Self. You will need to slow down and witness yourself operating from a different perspective and clarity through your own Higher Realm dimensional spaces.

You will still be *in* the third-dimensional world, just not *of* this third-dimensional world.

This entire evolutionary process involves anchoring your spiritual "knowing" within you, which entails you acclimatizing to the different energetic elements that will be operating through you. These elements are a part of your own spiritual makeup; they are not foreign but simply an aspect of yourself coming into active play. This anchoring phase is a necessary part of the plan for the full transformation and successful completion of the first level of your unfolding of Self.

The next phase is part of a sacred design of your own unfolding, which must be activated by you through conscious choice. As you stabilize and anchor your spiritual self through the physical body, your human aspect will go through a huge adjustment process. There will be a strong disorientation for the human part created by these new dimensional connections anchored through you. You will need to learn to navigate your way through life to a different rhythm within your experience in the moment. Within this totally unfamiliar energetic setting the human ego will need support to stabilize the emotional component of your human vulnerability.

It will be essential at this juncture of your process to bring the elements of your spiritual aspect to your human part. As you enfold the pure quality of love and compassion to that aspect of the human ego you can begin a conscious interpersonal connection with your human aspect. This process is about attending to an aspect of yourself, almost like a flowing bridge is created between your spiritual self and human aspect. This process of connection to support your human self is designed to end lifetimes of internal separation within you.

Tending to your self in this way allows a deeply needed healing process to take place within. This dynamic process will touch upon and permeate through all systems of your human self. The process will bring a peace and restfulness that have been desperately needed and sought by your human aspect for a long time.

Within this restorative state you will gain more clarity and effectively be able to integrate these new dimensional energetic alignments through your systems. This unfolding process within yourself will require a focused commitment by you and a willingness to enter the enormous love held within your sacredness of being. You will find with your new spiritual state that this process of unfolding becomes easy and deeply rewarding as you open into a sacred design that is held with your human aspect.

Old armoring will be able to fall away from the physical body through the energy of this love that you will be able to stabilize within you. Self-love will heal past wounds. The fear held in the physical body that was created through the illusions will be able to simply fall away. The fear will no longer be able to stay as Truth is held steady from your Higher Realm connections. All the density from the illusion will be able to dissolve.

The merging of your spiritual knowingness, to work directly with your human consciousness, is a sacred process. This brings truthful insights to your human conscious experience, and the love and compassion to all aspects of your third-dimensional journey.

You will find this a delightful process, bringing the Truth of the light back to your own humanness. Remember: Your human element has previously been weighed down by the restriction of illusion in this reality of the earth plane. You will begin a self-liberation process, releasing your human part from the guilt, shame; self-condemnation that has unfolded from the illusion lived. You will be able to bring the true perspectives of the same journey from the Higher Realms to the human element. This will be your own self-resurrection process that will set you free!

This process will require you to consciously open into an ongoing changing relationship with your human aspect. You will need to continue to be in the process of making a series of adjustments as you move even more deeply into this new frequency, allowing a merging to take place between both aspects of Self.

You came here to have a spiritual awakening and at the same time continue to have an evolving relationship with your human aspect. That is an aspect of the goal for all humankind and plays the part for the successful completion of your mission in this lifetime.

You have a deep innate desire within you, within your heart cells to wake up. Each one of you has this calling through an internal clock. This was the plan, the design, for you to awaken at this time. This awakening will allow you to begin to review your experiences in this lifetime so that you can witness the value of each individual "play out" that you have lived. You will be able to see the importance of each unfolding moment clearly, without the illusion in your way. Like players on a stage, each one of us is in the lead role in our own performance called life. You will perceive how each person around you has benefited from the "play out" created by you—how you have benefited from the play out of others. You will be the witness to the grand design held within the sacred synergy in your life.

Through this reflected Truth that you witness, you will be able to let go of more of the armoring you have placed around yourself. Through a series of introspection processes you will be able to see the truth of the courage that your human aspect has had moving through your many life experiences. This awareness usually takes place when you have completed your incarnation and left your physical body. In this lifetime, you will come into this clarity while still in your body, and begin a new way of life from this perspective of Truth.

As you move beyond the limitation of the veils you will find that you remember all that has been awaiting you. Through this you will easily begin to navigate into the new existence of Truth without illusion. You will begin to operate from this space as naturally as taking a breath.

We, the Pleiadians, are the "way showers" and it is our intention for you to fully awaken to these sacred aspects of Self. There is no time to lose for those of you who are ready. Being ready means that you are willing to let go and align back to who you are in Truth, beyond the veils. You only need to be willing to move beyond the third-dimensional drama. This drama is designed to hold illusion solidly in place. You will realign with your true sacred connections where you will join many others who are waiting for you beyond the veils. You will move into this sacred role once again, realigning back to your sacred reconnections.

You can come together with others who will also take their place. Jointly you will create a sacred synergy that will build a force of love here on your earth plane that has not been experienced before. Through this power of your collective Truth, through these sacred reconnections, much can be achieved on your planet. This frequency of your collective energy can touch humanity and bring about an accelerated state of awakening. You will collectively anchor this frequency of love that will have an energetic potency, creating a quickening through the hearts of humanity. You carry the keys to your own transformation on this earth.

Our role is to set this awakening in motion and then step back, allowing you to bring your own magic to your planet. That has always been the grand design. This awakening must stem from your own hearts, a collective love birthing through you.

The process described here is the unique signature of the "new dawning" energy in action. You will forge this profound, creative moment through the sacred, pure source connection of who you are collectively. This frequency of love can only be created through human interaction, by the action of united conscious choice. This energy only ignites through the combined spiritual human-chosen purpose. This happening will be unparalleled to all that has gone before within the Universe and will complete the anchoring of the New Dawning on earth.

This birthing of love between those of you who choose to join the Collective Oneness will create a fountain of light that will activate a series of new dimensional settings within the earth plane, creating the "new dawning of light." This brilliant light will open up a healing life force for all to receive on multidimensional levels, opening up the plains of creation. This light will support the shifts of consciousness on the planet, activating a destiny call to the next group who will be ready for their awakening.

The dense areas on the planet will begin to shift with this New Dawning energy created through the sacred synergy of your collective energies. This frequency energy will herald in an activation of change. There will be a proclamation for the time of a shifting of the balance between the light and the dark. The New Dawning light will take a form of movement across the planet, and each of you who are collectively involved will be holding the energetic Platform to secure and anchor the light frequency of this new balance between you.

There is a group of you who are destined to forge this collective reconnection now. You are in the first flow group, and then there will be many other collective soul groups that follow. This is the plan. This is going to be a sacred process that all of you will consciously share. This energy that you will collectively create will begin to activate a physical and energetic process of change on the planet. Your earth plane is set to hold a mirror carrying the dimensional frequency of change within its central Core, so the central Core carries the energy of the Imprint of this change of consciousness. The Core is holding that which is destined to take place through your own collective energies, carrying the mirror of the full Blueprint for this New Dawning energetic happening.

As you being to move through the veils and realign back to your natural sacred frequency, you will begin to transmit a pulse of your own frequency light through the physical cells of your body. This will align you to the Blueprint design of the Core within the earth. The Core will then begin to relate to and recognize your unique light frequency pulse through its own central mirror. The Core contains multidimensional realms of existence that are presently beyond the veils within your planet.

There will be a process set in motion as this is activated. The continual pulsing, like a heartbeat, will be moving from the central Core outward and across the planet. The pulsing is designed to strongly affect the dynamics of the third-dimensional process magnifying the illusion, the third-dimensional drama. Through this rapid shifting in the light frequency that will open within the planet, the density will become highlighted.

The frequency opening through the multidimensional layers, held within the physical planet, aligns you into other realities of Self that are living simultaneously. They are designed to realign you into different aspects of Self for a full integration of your own multidimensionality. They move outward into an unlimited space of timelessness and interact with the energetic field surrounding the earth.

This pulsing frequency will increase in intensity, bringing a complete transformation of the dimensional network within the energetic setting of the planet. This frequency is designed to gradually build up the magnetic energy within the planet's Core, which will ultimately transform the dimensional frequency on the planet, shifting the environment completely. Through this changing dimensional network, the planet will go through its own metamorphosis. It will return to its pristine state where the congestion of pollution will evaporate and be replaced by a clean transformed environment. There will be a rebalancing of Mother Earth, to mirror the energies of your own transformed consciousness. The natural forces will once again be uncompromised on your planet, as a new pure consciousness is held within the essence of nature.

This transformation of frequency will support the shifts of consciousness necessary for all human beings on the planet to awaken back to their natural state of being. This change in the dimensional frequency will create acceleration in the birthing process within the consciousness of humankind.

The shift of dimensional frequency will bring the awakening for many. They will simply awaken, like from a dream—the dream being this third-dimensional illusion of the experience of their lives lived on planet Earth. They will awaken from the dream and immediately remember themselves, their spiritual heritage. This will be a natural awakening. Those humans who are not ready for this transformation, who are not ready to let go of violence and the need to control others, will take their next step off the planet. Those human beings who are ready for this new experience of consciousness will take their next step on this planet.

When this process has completed, Planet Earth, which has been used to create this limited experience of the third-dimensional separation, will no longer exist for this purpose. Planet Earth will be transformed into carrying the completed New Dawning consciousness. This is the plan. This is the action of the plan. Nothing will stop this flow of change that is already in full motion.

Now you need to step forward and meet your Self. Take your place and open into your full experience of witnessing You in your power.

We, the Pleiadians, as part of the Universe, will be stepping back in order for you to have your own empowered experience. The truth is, only you as a human race can achieve the changes necessary for your earth plane to fully evolve.

We are with you as one consciousness throughout this whole process. We support you with the pure love of the Collective. We will witness you in your next steps to this key phase of your awakening. We hold you close as you recreate the magic between you and your planet Earth, between your humanness and spiritual self.

Through these upcoming chapters and the audio files we will reveal to you your pathway Home. There will be initiations to remove the filters and seals within you. There will be a weaving contained within these texts to assist you in your transition. We are committed to our role as part of The Promise to you.

Love and Blessings,
The Pleiadians

CHAPTER 1
OUR EARTH PLANE

There are new elemental energies opening up on our earth plane for the expressed purpose of assisting us in the next phase of our awakening. We need to comprehend an aspect of this new energetic format that is being launched on our planet. This understanding will support us in our ability to consciously and actively interact through this series of sacred designs, enabling us to fully participate within the unfolding processes. At first you may feel confused as you read about the energetic forms of consciousness that exist. As you begin to have a direct experience, as you engage with these energetic elements, you will start to perceive the different signature energies. This is our time to move beyond "not knowing" and to open up our hearts to this individual unfolding process through these sacred tools.

A pure form of brilliant light carrying the transformation of this time begins to flow onto the earth plane, heralding a celebration of this next stage of the New Dawning era. This sacred light carries the mirror of our unique brilliance and holds the purity of our light steady so that we can slowly realign to the full potential of our own sacredness. Through the mirroring of this brilliance we are being guided, slowly repositioned to our own light. We are being revealed to our selves. This light is designed to bring each one of us a sacred anointing. This gentle pure force is moving toward those of us who are ready to consciously receive. This light is automatically received within each individual consciousness.

The Sun is moving into another phase of its evolution and is opening up to birth a new level of consciousness through its brilliance. The Sun's mission at this juncture is to hold a mirror of its own brilliance, reflecting and transmitting the sacred heavenly energies to humanity. Simultaneously it is transforming the natural forces on the earth plane through its sacred touch.

The potential of our planet is being revealed through the pure flow of light rays reflected from the Sun. They are being radiated, deeply impacting the planet as it is being cradled by this holy consciousness.

The authentic design of the Sun's light rays mirroring is to reveal the depth of the layers of our own spiritual Self within us. As we consciously open to receive the reflections of the Sun's rays, there will be a quickening, an awakening taking place within our heart cells. The energy from the Sun's reflections creates an action of a multidimensional mirroring. This energy form is designed to release any density within any physical space, so there is a forceful letting-go process that naturally takes place within us.

The old armoring and density that has been held within our physical body for lifetimes will simply fall away. The sabotaging patterns created from the illusions of the third-dimensional reality that have been keeping us locked in a cycle, preventing us from being free to manifest, can now finally be released. This powerful letting-go process is essential to our awakening.

The wheel turns. The next phase of our journey has begun, as we are realigned to the vibrations of Self, returning Home. We will now be able to hold our illumination energy within us, enabling us to take this next step on our destiny path.

Our earth plane is on the brink of an evolutionary shift. This is a sacred moment. A new brilliance is about to shine upon us. We, as human beings, will take our places like never before in the history of the planet. The winds of change are heralding in, anchoring sacred forms onto our shores, carrying a birthing of consciousness to empower us to complete this next phase of our evolution.

The Truth is, our own hearts hold the full connection to our humanity and to our powerful spiritual nature. Through our sacred synergy we carry the potential to fulfill the prophecy of self-realization for the planet. Through the potency of who we are, individually and collectively, we will complete the prophecy that has been written.

Each one of us present is playing a part in what is being referred to by the Universe as "the Sacred Quest." Each one of us has been accepted to incarnate on this planet for this special mission. We each play a unique, individual role in this Quest to bring about the transformation of consciousness to humanity on the planet.

This plan has been set in motion on our earth plane through the anchoring of a Hologram of light. The Hologram has been formed by the God conscious creation element within the Universe. It is designed to act as a container, like a womb, that holds the full completion energies of our Quest. Through this Hologram there has been the activation of a sacred Covenant to bring about this divine happening. This Covenant creates, and holds, a holy forging between heaven and earth. This has never been seen before in the history of the planet. Through this forging, we on Earth are being given the grace to move beyond the illusion, beyond where we have existed, to align and begin to play our role within our own sacred aspect.

A Column of Light has birthed within the Hologram. The Covenant energy uses the Column of Light as a vehicle to create the heaven and earth connection. Like a bridge, this will enable us to more easily navigate our way through the illusion on the earth plane and align to the Higher Realm aspects of Self. We will be able to anchor the light of our Higher Self through our physical bodies and into the cells of our heart.

As we align to the light rays of the Sun, we will automatically become interconnected through this Column of Light. Remember: This will support us in stabilizing our own heavenly body aspect. There is a holy imprint anchoring on the earth plane from the Higher Realms through this Column of Light.

Within this Imprint is the design for the sacred anointing to take place within us. This holy energy will support many of us as we complete our essential sequences of awakening, which have been preordained to take place in this lifetime. The light of this Imprint shines brightly upon each one of us, aligning through our heart cells, propelling us forward to align to our destiny path.

This design from the Column of Light anchors the God Consciousness Group Mind space onto our planet and will facilitate us linking naturally into the Group Mind connection. This anchoring will lead into a completion of an aspect of our mission that we have promised to fulfill in this lifetime.

Another powerful aspect of this Covenant is the resurrection energies of Jesus Christ and Mother Mary. Yes, they have both played significant roles over a series of lifetimes. However, at this juncture they will begin an acceleration of their mission for us on the planet. They will become much more accessible to us on an individual level, and bring their initiations of love to support us in the completion of our mission. This support will take the form of a series of direct experiences with them. We will align to the reflected light that they carry, and through their presence we will meet our own state of Being.

These Masters are able to hold a Platform for each one of us that carries the energy of self-resurrection. They hold a mirror containing the vibrational frequency of the sacred heart that will create a recalibration of our heart cells, which enables us to move into a higher vibration of love than ever before. This action will support each one of us in being able to hold the pure frequency of love, and be that love.

These sacred activations will be endowed to us, as we are individually ready to receive them. This process is a sacred anointing by the Holy Spirit through Jesus Christ. We are to return, through our resurrection process, back to the whole. Through the pure love of Christ, we will once more transform ourselves and become spiritual beings. We are having a human experience while moving consciously in alignment to our own sacred divine aspect. These Masters carry the teachings of love and transmit a pure form of Truth. As we begin to enter this sacred time, we will consciously Be, and receive the gifts that have always existed, have always been within us.

The Continued Plan

At the right moment, those of us who are ready will come together, merging within the pure dimensional frequency that we individually hold. Collectively, we will carry this mirror of awakening for the rest of humanity. Those of us who are awake will be entrusted with holding this Platform for others to follow. We will hold the alliance of the Collective Consciousness within us to fulfill all phases of the process to bring the prophecy of this time to completion.

There are many of us who are on an awakening path in this lifetime. Each one of us carries the vibration of Truth within the cells of our heart. We already hold the developed unique frequency signature of our own divine creation element. Each one of us has, and is doing, our own inner work. Through an innate understanding of our mission, we are being directed through our heart cells in the form of an energetic pulse that we follow. This pulse creates a deep desire within us to express our innermost purpose. Each one of us is being compelled to move forward now, no matter what! We find ourselves being propelled into key roles to support the transformation of the planet and humanity. We are being asked to move forward and trust, not knowing how or where the next step is taking us. Each one of us is being strategically positioned, on a physical and an energetic level, throughout the planet. The repositioning is also taking place on many multidimensional levels within us.

While we may not understand or know all the details of the plan, it is essential to continue to let go and trust the unfolding moments that are before us. We take one step at a time as our Higher Self guides us. We are all being supported by the Collective Group Mind, which exists within the Universe of which we are a part. These energies are always available for us. We show up and consciously participate in this transformative step.

The heavenly guidance is contained within the Hologram and is transmitted through the Column of Light, supporting us in our alignment to our individual pathways. Remember: The Covenant energy holds the full energy of our awakened path and carries the sacred synergy for us. Within this sacred design there is a certain moment for many of us to begin a natural merging, forming a collective frequency of consciousness, a sacred synergy of light. We will still hold our own unique frequency within the

One, and find that we are more defined within our own uniqueness within the One. Each of us is like a unique jigsaw piece fitting perfectly into a puzzle. Together we create the full picture, the full synergy of light. This is a natural process. We are all part of the Collective God Consciousness Group Mind.

An Imprint is able to come from the heavenly plane and open up on the earth plane through the Column of Light, creating a sacred awakening of the multidimensional energy within the cells of the heart. The frequency of these dimensional settings opens up an alignment that will expand through the heart cells. It is through this that we can become energetically ready to hold the Higher Realm energies within the physical framework of our bodies.

As a collective awakened group, we are known as the "way showers." We have birthed into our human form to experience the illusion held on this earth plane. The plan now is for our full emergence by transcending the illusion here and moving back into a place of Truth. We are able to come from the depth of our illusionary experience on a human level and reach the full alignment to our sacred natures.

Each one of us had a beginning path, a story we have connected to and been able to relate in our humanness. Initially we needed the framework of our story in order for us to fully play out our experiences. This allowed us to have a reference point, from where we were within that story, and to emerge into having a full human experience.

At some moment in our individual stories we begin to slowly move beyond the illusion, to find and experience an aspect of our sacred nature. We begin to open into a self-revelation process that moves us into aspects of an authentic and sacred place, to gain back our wisdom. This is the first phase of the plan of our journey here.

Within our individual story lines there are great teachings. We can witness the rise of our own depth of feeling and through this we are given a unique opportunity to unfold, to feel passionately alive. As we are held in the grip of the illusion, we get to have a range of emotional experiences such as pain, struggle, isolation, grief, abandonment, shame, and rage.

Once we become deeply entrenched within these feelings they become a catalyst for our growth, bringing us closer to reaching our own higher potential within. We are able to then witness ourselves by opening into the vastness of our courage and our huge capacity to love. This is the grand design, created by us to evolve through our humanness so that we come to understand the vulnerabilities of our human aspect within our story.

We have been exposed to a wide range of illusion that exists here on the planet. Wherever our story has taken us, we have been the creator, the master of this grand design of our human experience. It is essential for us to open into the Truth of our journey that we have set in place in this lifetime. It is important to fully receive and acknowledge our own unique creation. As we examine what we have set in place for our self, we can fully utilize all the teachings contained within those experiences. Maybe even now we can open to more teachings that can be processed from past experiences. This whole journey of our story is a sacred process that we set in motion for our own transformation. We have given our selves these direct experiences to transcend through our human process.

There have been no accidents or wrong decisions made within our journey. Everything that has taken place within our life has been held through an impeccable sacred timing, for us to have our ultimate experience in the moment. This has been a perfectly orchestrated process to bring us to "all that we are" in this moment. We are the collective sum of our experience.

This journey brings us many experiences that take us into a place of separation. This separation occurs through the judgments and misperceptions of illusion from the ego-mind creating self-condemnation; judgments of how we have lived, of the decisions we have made, of our actions. This self-condemnation has created tremendous separation within us!

One aspect of the illusion that has been playing out strongly in this incarnation is the experience of feeling small and insignificant. We have had the feeling that we do not matter, we do not count, and that we cannot possibly make any difference within the world. We have created scenarios in our life to mirror this belief. The acceptance of our powerlessness has held us in a place of disconnection to our sacred Self.

For some of us there has been a strong experience of being a victim. There has been a huge framework of energy created by society that has held this illusion in place. Many of these rules of society have been anchored and held in place for lifetimes. Structured norms like doing the right thing, being responsible for others, being like everyone else, not being different and not celebrating our uniqueness. This includes going along with the group mentality and morality, accepting the non-existence of magic in the world. We have chosen to be suppressed and depressed by these unwritten laws.

We have been entrenched in the biggest illusion that exists only here on the earth plane: time. Within this illusion of time there is a strong feeling that this journey is endless. In truth our collective experiences here on this earth plane have been just one moment.

Transcending through the illusion can move us into simple Truths. We have done the best we could in each moment. We came here to this planet to have a series of experiences in order to learn. This moves us into a deep appreciation of all that we have allowed within each moment, honoring our selves for the courage we have had just being here to have our human experience.

By opening up and accepting Truth we are able to create a shift within our dimensional perspective of all that we are in this moment. At some point we will awaken to Self, and this whole experience of life will be like a dream. We will simply remember.

Finally, this experience of illusion is coming to an end. We are about to embark on a journey beyond the veils. This is an exciting and exhilarating step for all of us on the path. We are going to be liberated from the vastness of the illusions that have been operating here.

A next step of the journey is simply to witness the perspective of where we have been in our life up to this point. It is time to open to the truth of the energy of the many limitations that we have been operating within for most of this incarnation. Witness this Truth, accept all the learning processes, and let go. We have all needed this human experience within the third-dimensional illusion creating separation from our sacred nature. This whole journey of illusion is now obsolete and has served its purpose. Our reason for being here on the planet has changed.

Now is the time to move into the next phase of our experience. We are no longer here to have this limited human experience within this illusion. Instead, we are being opened into the new energy on the planet, assisting us in aligning back to our original authentic spiritual nature.

This is our time to make a shift in consciousness through a self-resurrection process. This is our time to reclaim our natural spiritual heritage. Many of us have already started this process of moving beyond the limited illusion. Through this dramatic energetic shift on the planet a further acceleration of our own birthing and awakening process is guaranteed. There is the destiny realized for the planet and all humanity. The prophecy written for our sacred quest is happening now.

We are each being held within the sacred Covenant and awakened through the Imprint that has been anchored through the Column of Light coming onto the planet. Through these sacred energies we are being held and anointed to realign to the light of ourselves. The Pleiadians are holding these new energetic components, which are part of this New Dawning energy. This is the official end to our being held within the illusion on this planet. Our human experience of limitation is over.

The Pleiadians are creating a steady vibrational frequency for each one of us to make our transition. They work side by side with the energy of Jesus Christ, Mother Mary, the Galactic Community, and the Spiritual Realms for our collective awakening. This next step involves birthing a bridge from our human element to our spiritual being. This bridging involves opening into simple Truths. First, we need to open into a state of acceptance, honoring our human journey. This is accomplished by our willingness to witness the full story we have lived in this lifetime, and letting go.

Next we need to own the full creation of our life. This allows us to claim full receivership of all our experiences. Through this ownership we can then let go of any aspect of feeling like a victim, or moving into self-blame, or self-condemnation. As we receive the Truth of our life being created perfectly for us and by us, we can then let go and receive our self fully. As we move into this process of self-acceptance, self-love follows as a natural state.

Accepting all aspects of our journey brings to an end any internal separation, which is essential in order to navigate our way through to a successful integration between our humanness and spiritual self. The process of self-acceptance promotes self-love and allows us to hold and activate the full frequency of our self-realization potential for enlightenment.

We have suffered enough.

There is a "calling" frequency, likened to an "echo," that originates from the heavenly body of pure consciousness. This sacred movement works through the Column of Light and is then sourced through the light of the Sun's rays. The frequency contained within the echo kisses the earth plane, touching all life force. Humanity is able to naturally absorb the mirroring of this pure consciousness into the heart, interacting directly through the heart cells. This echo allows a transfer of our own divine light to begin to birth through us, aligning us directly into Truth. Our own light has the capacity to nourish us on a deep level. This access to our authentic light creates the opening, a natural access point, to our place beyond the veils.

You will find: *You are who you have been waiting for.* Now is the time for us to realign to our place of origin. As we begin this phase of our journey, we will be incorporating our spiritual being with our human aspect. This has always been the plan. The Hologram of Light will be fulfilled as we each step forward and own our sacred reconnections to Home through the sacred Column of Light. Our own promise to Self is fulfilled within our heart.

Through this anchoring of Heaven and Earth energies on the planet the bridge is forged for all time. As we become the catalyst for our own transformation, we can then hold the anchor steady, through the Column of Light, for the rest of humankind in their self-resurrection.

We will not do this alone.

Note: You can find an audio file link at *www.christinedayonline.com/pleiadianpromise* This will align you to the Hologram, and to the Column of Light to support your transitional alignment to Self.

CHAPTER 2

THE HOME SPACE

Each one of us on the path is beginning to move into this next phase of our unfolding, which is designed to align us to our higher purpose. We are to emerge like a butterfly from our cocoons, holding within us our Origin design that carries the full patterning of our multidimensionality. Our higher purpose is carried within this sacred design, which engages with the Higher Realm connections to our unlimited potential, for us to emerge into a greater part of our own multidimensionality of Self. We will begin to be repositioned back into the sacred alignments of our original place, within our own heritage state.

Our incarnation experience has been deeply immersed in the third-dimensional illusion, which has given us a very limited expression of our true potential as human beings. Now we are moving into a next stage of our unfolding that is designed for us to open into a different phase of experiencing our humanness through our capacity to have compassion and to love ourselves and others.

The formed Covenant holds this completed prophecy for this time. One aspect of the Covenant's role is to act as the energetic container, the womb. This womb is a stabilizer and holds an anchor for the Imprint of our sacred design, so that we can be self-realized. The frequency of our Imprint is carried within the Covenant and we are able to source it directly from our Home Space. The sacred design of our Imprint holds the completed Blueprint for this next phase. This awakened energy is the sacred aspect of Self.

The role of the Hologram is to hold a Platform, supporting us to be able to navigate to, and then enter, our Home Space. It acts as a mirror, which reflects the multidimensional settings of our Imprint. Each one of us will resonate to the Truth of what is being reflected out to us, within the unique energetic aspect of our Imprint. We will get to experience our individual role through the grand design that is projected by the Hologram of Light. Our Imprint essence pulses outward from the Hologram, sending out a call, an echo, that can be recognized and resounds in our Home Space. We are ready to unfold as energetic beings.

Let's look at how we are going to locate and open into our Home Space. Your Home Space is located within your physical heart area and extends across the whole space of your chest. This is simply the physical position. The doorway leads us beyond the illusion on the planet, into the natural link of our multidimensional, unlimited potential of our Higher Self. This is our Home Space.

Within our Home Space we have the capacity to enter what is called the Sacred Trust, which is an aspect of our Home Space. This is where all aspects of our self-mastery energies exist. Essential energetic gifts and tools are waiting to be received by us, as we are ready to receive them. We are to utilize these gifts and energies now in our current mission. These gifts of ours are designed to accelerate our awakening. Within our Sacred Trust we can enter our Mastery essence, unveiling that sacred aspect of Self that opens us into a series of realignments of our power. We are realigning, recollecting that which is ours!

The full frequency of our Mastery Self awaits us within the multidimensional container of our Home Space from within our Sacred Trust space. This is an important element of our journey Home, which requires a series of unveiling processes. It is our conscious choice to return back and reclaim that which is naturally ours. We access our Sacred Trust energy and then anchor the energetic aspect of Self, which we receive through the Home Space.

Our mission right now is to answer the call, transmitted from our Imprint held within the Hologram of Light. We will first be received and then we will begin our initiation back to the Higher Realms of light, re-birthing into our original form.

Our mission is to anchor our authentic light forms back through the cells of our heart within our Home Space and ultimately carry our full frequency of divine light within our physical body. Each one of us is to carry within us our unique form of light consciousness and become a living transmitter of light for the planet. Together, those of us on the path will rejoin the One. This is possible through our collective God consciousness aspect. The process is an aspect of the Prophecy. There is to be a natural forging of our collective sacred design imprint to be held between us. These combined Imprints will hold the frequency for transforming the consciousness of humankind. This is the plan.

We are ready to begin this next phase of our planet's history. We are being given the grace now, as the energies of the heavenly light flow through from the Hologram, through the Column of Light onto the planet. These vibrations are designed specifically to support us in this next phase of our transition. Many of us have completed this third-dimensional illusionary phase as human beings on the planet, and are being bestowed with these sacred energies of purity, designed to nurture and bless us. This is designated as the next phase of our awakening process.

Throughout this incarnation we have lived in a separated state from our Home Space. There have been no definitive instructions on how we would even begin to comprehend the energy and essence of our Self within the Home Space. With the lifting of many dimensional veils there has been a strong shift of the illusion on the planet. The lifting of the veils has been like a curtain coming up on a stage, and we will get to witness Truth, and begin to open back into a knowing, a remembering.

As the veils lift there are revelations. This unveiling allows us to begin to experience something new, to understand a Truth that brings to us a deeper sense beyond illusion. Through the clarity, specific directives will be revealed. We then will be able to open into a truer, more authentic aspect of ourselves and begin this journey back to Self within the Home Space. These shifts of awareness will open up opportunities to those of us who are ready to move into this next realm of consciousness.

The Hologram of Light will act as an anchor for this next level of transformation on the planet. The Hologram will hold the dimensional settings open that have been created through the lifting of the veils. The Hologram of Light will play an essential, ongoing role as a strong anchor for us as we begin this transformational process within our Home Space.

At this sacred time in our destiny we are being given full access to our Home Space. We are now ready. We have done our inner work. This initiation process will return us fully to all aspects of our Home Space and Sacred Trust. This is the beginning of our self-fulfilling Prophecy, which has always been held in place through the Covenant. This Covenant is being activated on the planet through the heavenly body held in place by the Hologram. This pure frequency of light that is held within the Covenant, anchors a fluidity that moves through the Hologram into us, which assists us in returning to our natural fluid, multidimensional state.

The anchored energy held by the Hologram holds a Platform for us. There is a sacred form held within the Hologram that supports our transition to our own Home Space. It will align us, enabling a smooth entry into our Home Space. There is a collective synergy between all: the Covenant, the Column of Light, and the Hologram. Each one of these individually and collectively supports our ongoing transition through our enlightenment journey within our Home Space.

The Sun continues to play an essential role in our transition. The Sun's reflective rays carry the mirrored fluidity of our brilliance. So it is necessary that we move into a state of receivership, actively opening up to the Sun's rays, drinking in the light, bringing this directly into our heart cells, into our Home Space. With this birthing of liquid light flowing into our Home Space we are able to merge more easily into the expanded dimensional fluidity. This sunlight fluidity is a natural component that moves through all dimensional layers within our Home Space. We are being invited to move beyond the disbelief, and open into the New Dawning light that is being imparted to us through the light rays of the Sun.

There is a strong letting-go energy that exists within the Home Space. Working with this energy will allow all of the old limitations to be brushed aside as we open to receive the sacred, which is rightfully ours. We can align freely into our entitlement, fully receiving our selves and moving effortlessly into this next phase of our transition.

The moment we enter our Home Space we are welcomed into a womb of light and become enfolded within this sacred process. One aspect of the Covenant is our returning to be received by the Collective Consciousness of the Group Mind energy. We are immersed and bathed within this consciousness light. This initiation of consciousness activates a deep, inner strengthening process within our own Spirit. Our spiritual essence rises up through us, bubbling to the surface. Like a rising sun, coming up over the horizon, the light rays of our spiritual being flow through our cells. We have always been a part of this Collective Consciousness and now, we consciously return.

Our journey begins within the Home Space, an ongoing, layered, conscious birthing process. There will be the focused meeting point of the multidimensional sacred aspect of our Higher Self, each one of us existing within each moment of our experience. Each one of us is expressed within our own unique divine frequency. Within that frequency we are everywhere, connected to all life force within the Collective Universes. Every aspect of our sacred nature is held within the One; we are an individual aspect of the Collective Group Mind Consciousness.

This is our journey as we occupy and activate the full multidimensionality of our sacred Home Space. As we are ready, there is a deep fulfillment awaiting us through the expression of the sacred love of our authentic Self in action.

The Pleiadians' role is to hold the multidimensional settings open for us as we make these series of sacred reconnections. Their support will enable us to fulfill the transition of each individual multidimensional initiation, to move into a self-realization process by utilizing and fully integrating these series of Higher Realm aspects of Self, and anchoring each level of the initiations within the cells of our physical body.

The Pleiadians oversee our entire metamorphic process, which carries a powerful life force creative energy that is fluid in nature. These frequencies weave themselves through the cells, and the cells go through an unfolding transmutation process. Through this process of transmutation, we will be constantly adjusted energetically as a new webbing structure is birthed within us. The sacred synergy moving through the cells allows a natural unveiling of our Master Self.

Within each unfolding moment the Pleiadians hold the aspect of us that is currently birthing, and in that moment of birth they place an energetic womb around us. This energetic womb creates a holding frequency that will allow a full integration of the higher aspect of our light to anchor through the cells of our heart. This process of support is essential to our unique unfolding process of awakening.

In this New Dawning time we will begin to appreciate and express our own multidimensional potential that exists within us. For lifetimes we have been working within a restricted Framework on this earth plane with just our third-dimensional human aspect. We have been locked into the components of our limited self and have been drawing from, and operating within, a singular energetic Framework.

Our Home Space is made up of many layers of singular Frameworks, each one being multidimensional in form. We will link into the individual settings through our Home Space. Each Framework setting expresses a multifaceted sacred element of our energetic being. Now is the time to begin to understand parts of our multidimensionality through a series of direct experiences. We will gain stronger clarity as we begin accessing the sacred elements that are contained within each Framework.

We know that our Home Space is made up of a series of individual Framework pieces and that an important part of our journey is to initiate through each one. Each piece of our Framework is a natural extension of our Self and exists as part of a multidimensional natural extension of our Home Space. Through each individual aspect of the multidimensional Framework is a series of what is called "light fragments." These light fragments carry the authentic part of Union, the state of communion that connects us all through sacred forms of the God Consciousness state.

As we access our multidimensional Framework and align through our light fragments, the communion energy of the God Consciousness Group Mind will begin a transmission of the One. The energy of the One will be another catalyst for the further activation of our Imprint design. This will create a deeper forging within our heart cells, creating a strong recalibration of electrical energy within our system. Our Imprint design sets off a profound inner process of awakening, like a clock mechanism. A process begins, awakening a transmitting frequency entering every cell within us, waking every cell to a new experience of being. Our cells are ready for this next step!

As our Imprint design begins to be forged through the heart cells, a quickening takes place, an acceleration of pure light opening, aligning us further to the God Consciousness. Our Imprint creates a repositioning of our DNA strands. This repositioning process begins to work through the pineal and pituitary glands that expand and activate our energetic makeup in the brain, opening up areas in the brain that have not been utilized in this lifetime. This shift within the brain includes a dimensional expansion of our sensory elements, and activates a new sacred sensory element within us. This Sense will be essential to our existence as we take our place within the Collective Group Mind setting. Until now, this Sense has been lying dormant.

As we align through your individual Framework levels within the Home Space our integration process through the light fragments is accelerated. This sensory activation is designed to bring us into a heightened experience of communion through the multidimensional interactions with the Collective Consciousness community.

This sensory awakening acts like a key to a door, opening a further empowerment to unfold within us. Through this awareness of our power there is a deep experience of Self that can emerge through us. This happening naturally filters through the heavenly light held by the Hologram and transmits out onto the planet. This forges a path of empowerment for others to follow, and impacts the earth plane on a profound level by changing the cycle that has existed for lifetimes.

This sensory expansion within is assisting to align us to higher frequencies of Truth. These Truths contain a pure existence of love within the Higher Realms. We need this aspect of the pure frequency of love to receive, integrate, and anchor the higher levels of our consciousness through our physical heart cells. The anchoring of this light frequency promotes self-love and in turn births a natural rejuvenation element to all the cells within our physical body.

The frequency of our unique Imprint design is potent, creating a recalibration right through every cell. Our DNA strands will continue with a repositioning process, shifting our entire energetic makeup within as we are energetically expanded and reconnected to the communion energy of the One.

As the expression of our Imprint design births we are able to take a fuller role within our place within the Collective God Consciousness. The full brightness and activation of our light frequency of the grand design unfolds, like a flower to the sun, within the flowing consciousness that exists within the One. Our bloom of light will create a massive response through the Universe. This event of aligning through our light fragments is a sacred motion that forges an aspect of our unique Imprint design. This creates the action of our own self-realization process of enlightenment.

The journeying experience through our Home Space gives us insights into a different way of being through our multidimensional Self, almost as though we are learning to navigate our way through new terrain. The shifting of our conscious awareness opens us into our natural fluid state, which allows us to utilize the different Time Lines that exist within the Higher Realms. The Time Line holds all experiences that have gone before and are to come. Time is the biggest illusion on our earth plane. As we enter through the Time Line, all experiences are available simultaneously, in the one moment that actually exists, the present. Through an unfolding within "the moment" we get to discover how to interact through our multidimensional Self, within this direct experience, entering a full fluid state of Truth.

Our thought processes will alter as we move into these higher frequencies of Truth. We are going to experience a changing energetic landscape in our world that is fluid in nature. This fluidity links through us as an extension of Self. As we come more within the union of our multidimensionality we will naturally disengage further from the illusion of the third-dimensional energy on this planet. This alignment through the multidimensional design Framework of Self has an unlimited potential from which we can source. Our own consciousness transforms as we align further through the collective God Consciousness community within this fluid state of birthing.

For some of us, an aspect of our mission here is to work within this expanded webbed Framework, supporting the birthing of a new consciousness on the planet. This Framework plays a significant role in supporting the energetic transformation of the natural elements, to bring nature back to its original pristine state. Realize that the Blueprint for this energetic setting of nature still exists and in the correct moment, this Blueprint will activate and reset the natural energies within earth. This activation and reset will be accomplished through our individual participation within our own evolved Framework. This will be supported by the formation of many energetic ley lines and the restoration of multidimensional settings that have already begun to take place for the transformation of all life that exists on the planet.

We have been operating from a very limited perspective within the natural environment on the earth plane to this point in our evolution. As we begin our evolving process we will discover the many expanded multidimensional elements that exist within the Shamanic worlds that are connected through the natural forces. Through the transformation of our own dimensional energetic settings much will be revealed as we experience this deepening of our connections to nature. An essential aspect of our enlightenment process is developing sacred and intimate relationships within the natural forces, and strong allies with the natural forces.

The Covenant holds a dynamic frequency that is pure, and is held within a unique vessel in the form of a Template. This Template carries a sacred force of light that unfolds an ancient mystery that has not previously been witnessed in this form. This is a raw power that is to be activated through an ordination by God in the presence of the Covenant. A sacred space has been created, like a container, to carry this powerful and transformative source of what the Pleiadians are calling the "WE" energy.

The WE holds aspects of the sacred, mysterious authority of God. We have always had a direct alignment with this omnipotent consciousness. This has been so since the beginning of time. Our awareness of this Truth has not yet been fully realized through our cells in the form of a direct experience.

Moving forward through this sacred process of realignment through the Template of the Covenant, we begin to be drawn like a magnet within that all-pervasive WE energy. This WE energy dimensionally and energetically reaches far beyond the I AM creation energy. The WE energetic frequency carries the pure sacred essence of creation that permeates through our very existence, moving beyond our expression of anything known. The WE is containing the full understanding of love held by God. This holding of this divine love is being kept for us until we can carry it ourselves. This vibration of love is far beyond anything we have encountered thus far in this lifetime within our heart, and will transcend all restrictions, all limitations. This love is all encompassing. The fullest understanding of Truth is revealed within this sacred form. The Covenant holds the frequency of this unlimited potential for all to unfold within.

Our energetic and physical systems need to transform for us to be able to carry and anchor this full vibrational light of the WE frequency. The physical systems of our body will need to go through a complete metamorphic transformation and birth into a new electrical system in order to hold the pure WE frequencies. An aspect of this energetic acceleration will be the new design of our system through the expansion of our crystalline structure that is held within our heart cells, thyroid, brain, and full spine. Our crystalline structure has the potential to hold the full hierarchy of these sacred frequencies.

The crystalline structure was birthed through every human being on this earth plane on 11/11/11. The crystalline structure is located in the space between the cells of our physical body. Now this structure will play the role of opening into a powerful dimensional setting within our body systems, enabling a current of electrical light to flow through us. This crystalline structure will be able to hold the fullness of the purity through the WE energy and is also designed to act as an integrator for this pure love element that is held for us by God.

Once aligned through the crystalline structure, this form of the WE energy can be consciously held and transmitted outward to humanity. As we hold and become part of the WE energy our role changes within us. As the potential carrier, we become a natural extension of our aspect of God. This is part of the plan for those of us who are holding the path for others to follow. We become sacred transmitters of this profound force of love.

Our awakening is to fulfill and complete the Prophecy in this lifetime. The Prophecy is that we anchor heaven on earth through the WE vibration within us and transmit this outward on the planet. The Prophecy is self-fulfilling. We open into our fully awakened Higher Self carrying the complete vibration of the WE, the love of God anchored alive within our physical body.

The truth of the One is fully expressed within the vibrational form of the WE. This frequency holds the purest and most sacred aspect of the One. The WE carries the full form of a golden, fluid light consciousness that is uplifting by the vibration of Truth that it contains. The golden light's role is to impart to each one of us our full Homecoming design that is sacred in nature. This design has been created, and anchored in a Hologram form of a Blueprint before we entered this earth plane. The WE, also known as the sovereign energy, is designed to activate our higher sacred rite of passage. It holds the sacred Covenant of our God aspect that has existed within us for all time.

This is the moment for many of us to return to the WE energy. The Truth that is carried within this energy needs to be revealed through the spoken word. There is power within the spoken word. An aspect of the Prophecy is the necessity for the "Word of the WE" to be activated by us, through our own unique sound. Our frequency sound creates a fulfillment, opening us up into a full self-realization process. This awakening energy is to be anchored onto the earth plane through each one of us.

Within this unique frequency of our sound of the word, there is a sacred light activation opened up within our heart cells. We get to fulfill an aspect of our own Prophecy as we bring our sound of the word to be made manifest within the Universe. The pure, golden energy of the word becomes even more fully realized on the earth plane, creating a further birthing element within this New Dawning energy. There is an essential happening in the moment as we take in the frequency created by our unique sound. We need to breathe, and open into this anchoring energy, and allow a golden multidimensional form to be woven through our heart cells.

The WE energy transforms the energetic moment of Truth to a new dimensional paradigm. The Truth, within the golden space of our Self, is the magnificent, unlimited light in form. The WE is the glorious God element, beauty revealed within the sacred center of each heart cell. WE are!

An important part of our role as we awaken is to work within these multidimensional elements on this planet, and learn to stabilize and create from our Master space through the exalted platform of the WE. We forge a path for others to follow through our own higher awakening of our God aspect.

As we become our Home Space, a great awakening is made manifest through us, giving us access to the multifaceted aspects of our Master Self. These profound series of initiations activate energetic extensions of Self and these extensions unveil the revelations of this New Dawning era through us.

The Pleiadians make the necessary adjustments and continue to monitor our energetic settings. This is a necessary process as we each adjust to the series of new multidimensional settings and activations that are made manifest within us.

As we fully initiate into the Home Space, there are many sacred realms that we will rejoin—that we will reconnect. We are part of the Collective, an aspect of the One, an aspect of the golden dawning of the WE.

One facet of the completion phase of our journey within the Home Space is our awareness of the necessity for a constant, continual energetic adjustment phase. This is essential for our full transmutation process within our physical form. There will be a series of ongoing activations opened up through us. These will unveil in-depth understandings of higher-evolving consciousness, which will be imparted through the sacred design of our Master Self that exists within our fully self-realized Home Space.

As adjustments through our consciousness take place we are able to enter a higher purpose within the golden light of the WE through our Home Space. Know there are many shifts of consciousness that will create new perceptions of reality that we have not previously experienced.

I would liken this sacred unfolding, unveiling, to being in a darkened room, only seeing part of the space in shadow, and suddenly the Sun shines into the room creating illumination. There are many incredible forms and sacred ways of being that exist within us. We are now ready to receive ourselves, to begin the sacred event of self-revelation.

We move into a self-empowerment process as we align through the knowledge that exists within our Home Space. Aligning to that knowledge reveals deep insights that hold Truth and this frequency of Truth will begin to flow and merge within us. We will begin the sacred path that carries the beauty and the fluidity of light of this time, within the container that is each one of us. This is the moment for us to begin to navigate our way through the extensive Framework that we are, moving back to the level of freedom through Truth being revealed.

WE are the light. We are the light. The light fragment exists through every setting, carrying a life force frequency that magnifies and reflects Truth. Truth exists within the frequency of our heart cells, our Home Space, which is a multidimensional unit that exists within our heart cells. Each heart cell holds a frequency of Truth that can propel us into a state of the pure existence of the WE love. This love carries the multidimensionality of our being and will be expressed through us in the sacredness of the moment.

WE are the moment. WE are the sacredness of the moment. When we use the words I AM we begin to align, we begin to claim that frequency which is held within the light fragment. This is our moment to come Home to our full expression of Self. This is a pure force connection element of us fusing in light. WE..., WE..., WE... the heart cells begin to pulse forth a golden multidimensional frequency of light that contains the full Truth of love. We are love. We are the golden God energy in motion.

This deep shifting activation of birthing our multidimensional perception will open us up to a new purpose for Being. This unveiling has been withheld until now, simply because it has not been the time for humanity to take this step until this very moment. Those of us on the awakening path are ready to forge this connection into our unique Home Space.

Our journey Home is being celebrated! We are being received back to our place with great appreciation, joy, and thanksgiving!

Note: You can find an audio file link at *www.christinedayonline.com/pleiadianpromise* You will work with this audio file to connect to your Home space. Let go and allow the fullness of your journey.

The Pleiadians are committed to working with each of you as you take this conscious and powerful next step.

Enjoy the journey!

CHAPTER 3

THE COLLECTIVE GROUP MIND

The Collective Group Mind is the woven creation of God. The breath of God birthed a creation life force element through the Universe and the Collective Group Mind was made manifest. This was the life force creation of a holy action by God. The Collective Group Mind structure is the full form creation light energy of God that has always existed since the forming of the Collective Universes.

This Group Mind structure, made from the breath of God, is a pure, sacred, multidimensional consciousness. The God creation element is a fluid weaving that births the sacred elements through the Collective Group Mind. We are each organically linked to this fluid form. Each of us has a unique placement within this consciousness and we play an original role within the Collective Group Mind. God nourishes the Collective Group Mind and breathes the life force essence of creation, opening a vibrational consciousness that interconnects directly within the entire Group Mind. This essence of creation exists through all time, weaving its consciousness to all life force energy groups—flowing outward to each life force element within the Universe, creating a divine webbing network.

Our origins began within the sacred structure of the Collective Group Mind. Each one of us is like a seed planted beneath the soil in a garden of light, and the light of God nourished each individual, like the Sun. Each one of us was opened, like a flower to the Sun, and at that very moment of our spiritual birth the pure frequency of God entered us. That element of God as consciousness has taken root within our hearts cells. We are able to access this element of our spiritual birth within our Imprint through our Home Space. We have the fullness of the experience within us. This is an empowering moment that can be accessed when we are ready to experience the expansiveness of the love.

Through the omnipresence of the Collective Group Mind, our own pure spiritual self has had a permanent anchor, a place where we can play out the full potential role of our spiritual originality. Where we exist as a unique aspect of the One, this is our Spiritual Home.

A Message to You From the Collective Group Mind

Sacred being of light, we call to you.

We witness you as an aspect of the One, an aspect of the Group Mind consciousness. We acknowledge your journey thus far and invite you to re-enter your place consciously at the sacred juncture of this time. All awaits each one of you within the moment. As you re-enter the Collective in the moment, know that no time has passed since you left. We witness you and remind you of your place that has remained unchanged through the eons.

There is a frequency time frame change on your planet now as the veils have lifted, a path has been lit so that you can move forward and consciously rejoin us. We are here and you are here. We are joined in consciousness through the God connection, in this unfolding moment of Truth. There will be the moment that you choose consciously to reconnect within the Truth, for there is only one Truth.

The opening of the moment of Truth is here for you. The veils have lifted for you to come and fully take your place consciously within the

Collective Group Mind. This conscious reconnection to your place within the Collective Group Mind is a major component to activating this second phase of your process. This is you rejoining that of which you have always been a part.

This will be a "turn of the wheel" in your enlightenment, for you to be revealed within the Knowledge and open into the depth of your Sacred. This Truth is held within the moment and there is only one moment in time that you have ever existed within. You return to exist within "the moment."

We bring to you the teachings that have been passed down through the ages, ancient texts that contain the Truth and understandings held within all time, within the moment. You are a part of this teaching of Truth that exists. You hold within your cells an aspect of the sacred design of the texts. And as you carry this energy of the sacred design within your Imprint we are able to impart to you the full frequencies that are held within these holy passages.

As we present to you the full frequency that is carried within that which is sacred, you will begin to awaken and arise consciously into your place within the Collective Group Mind. These frequencies that we bring to you will naturally guide you deeper within the energetic folds of our Collective energy, enabling you to flow and anchor through the multidimensional layers of the Group Mind consciousness. As you move deeper and deeper within the Collective you will shed all old concepts, belief systems, and misperceptions. Only that which is holy within you will remain.

This is your time to resurrect another aspect of your spiritual content within, to reach through your Home Space and begin the journey of reconnection to the Collective Group Mind. Your initial entry point will be your Home Space, and this space will act as a doorway for you to begin a returning. Here you will access your next turn in the road. You will move forward to remember and then to reclaim that which is the holy purity of your God aspect. This signature is a part of your natural design that is held within the Higher Realm aspects of your Imprint.

Your original design carries a multidimensional fluidity and is multifaceted in nature. The frequency of the sacred design of your Imprint is what allows you to be that unique aspect within the Collective Group Mind consciousness. You are recognized through your own divine Imprint and your frequency forms an essential aspect of the Collective Group Mind energy. You are part of this sacred synergy of God that exists within our Collective Consciousness. This is your time for a conscious returning, for you to come and receive a self-fulfillment within your own heart, as it has been preordained in the sacred texts.

Know that an aspect of your Higher Self has always been aligned to the Collective Group Mind and this connection has always been maintained since the beginning. Moving within the sacred connection allows for your self to transition on yet another level through the process of conscious choice into the understanding that your place does exist within the Collective Group Mind. This acceptance by you begins the next phase of your conscious realignment to the Collective Group Mind.

Now it is the time for you to begin this path, to consciously awaken and move into an expanded experience of consciously rejoining the Collective Group Mind. To embark on a glorious journey as you open into the vastness of your light that exists within your place, consciously aligning to the sacred transmissions as a multifaceted aspect of the Collective Group Mind.

The first step to begin your journey of reconnection is to accept the Truth that your place exists within a multidimensional framework within the Collective Group Mind. As you move toward this acceptance there will be a quickening that begins to activate within your individual place within the Collective Group Mind. Through your acceptance this sacred space will transmit an energetic frequency pulse that will move you, guide you toward your sacred space within the Collective Group Mind.

Simultaneously as you open into this energy of acceptance, there will be an activation response within an area of your brain, a reopening of a receptor that will link you directly into this sacred space within the Group Mind frequency settings. This sacred connector within your brain will begin to align you to a multidimensional expression of light that is part of the Group Mind. Through this gradual building of this expression of pure light from the Group Mind communion there will be an awakening, an illumination, a sudden recognition of the sacred presence that has always existed within you.

Through the passageway that links the receptor in your brain to the Group Mind you will be moved through a series of multidimensional openings that will give you access into the moment of transition. You will be called to surrender in this moment. This is a requirement at that pivotal moment of reconnection. This is where you begin to blend into a holy reunion, forming a sacred synergy. This transition will be a turning point, as you reopen into the sacred, into "the moment." We are waiting to receive you.

Our Group Mind process is designed in a multidimensional, layered form that encompasses the entire Universes. This layered consciousness that we are, exists through every life form within the entire vista of the Universes and is all pervasive, all seeing. An aspect of our role is to hold the consciousness of light and transmit this steadily outward for all to receive. At this juncture, we the Group Mind have created the Covenant that is holding the Hologram in place on your planet. This Hologram is designed to support the transformational settings that are working through each one of you for this next phase of your awakening. Be aware that you too are holding this Blueprint as part of the Group Mind consciousness. Your Higher Self is actively engaged within the Group Mind with this unfolding journey.

We, the Collective Group Mind, are able to receive you on a more authentic level as you open up your intention to align. We can totally embrace you within the full spectrum of the multidimensional moment that exists. This will also be supported within an unlimited framework that is held within the moment, where everything is in a state of Being. Within this state everything exists simultaneously. Through this pure state you will begin to fully recognize and remember that which is Truth. We can meet you authentically within the elements of this Truth. This state of Being creates a strong base of love where all things exist and arise through a pure reality. This will be our meeting point with you.

This container that we are, carries Truth. We hold a mirror reflecting the full force of love throughout the Universes. This love is what fuels the Universes. It matters not whether it is individually utilized, because it exists regardless of any individual action. This purity is designed to support all life force.

You left this moment, this meeting point, when you came onto the planet for this incarnation. Now you are ready to return fully to this Collective Group Mind energy. This process, your journey that you have been experiencing on planet earth, has been a very short span of time in reality. Your return is monumental and glorious because this time you will return with your human form intact. Previously the only way possible for you to return was in spirit form. This changing dynamic is made possible because of the New Dawning era and through your newly transformed electrical system that has been birthed within the physical cells of your body. You now carry the full potential to hold all the energetic elements necessary to enter and stabilize within your place of the Group Mind.

This whole process is part of the Prophecy that is waiting to be fulfilled by you playing your role in realigning to the frequency of your place within the Collective Group Mind. This reconnection to the Collective Group Mind activates a creation element that accelerates a state of passage and opens up a huge wave of light consciousness on your earth plane. This is a frequency of consciousness that will build in momentum across the planet, impacting the essential elements in activating this second phase of the New Dawning energy. This action by you will fulfill the Prophecy of making manifest the frequency of "heaven on earth" that will unfold and come to pass through an opening being initiated within each individual who is ready to receive this awakening.

This entire process will herald in a vibrational frequency of light consciousness to be made manifest on the planet. Your reconnection to the Group Mind will create a dynamic new cycle of awakening to be birthed within you, and at the same time, shift the cycle of limitation on the earth plane. Your reconnections will forge an energetic Blueprint path for others to follow. This process will transform the energetic settings on your earth, as the magnetic Core energy will shift opening a multidimensional Time Line that will launch this transitional phase on another level.

This is an energetic happening that has never before taken place on the earth plane. This action creates a unique awakening cycle for human kind, and can be likened to "the phoenix rising out of the ashes." This is a resurrection energy that is incredibly significant for the ongoing progress of the awakening for mankind.

This metamorphic process will be supported through the Hologram of Light that is being held by the Covenant. This process of awakening is stabilized through the energy of the Covenant. The Hologram acts as a mirror reflector enabling the full awakening of Truth as the Covenant works directly through the Collective Group Mind consciousness.

Much of the Knowledge that is housed within the Collective Group Mind has been hidden within a multidimensional sacred form. Until recently you have been immersed in the third-dimensional illusion of separation from Truth. This has served the purpose for you to have your full experience of limitation of being human on this planet. Now there is a shift in direction because you have accomplished all that you came here to do in this first phase of experience on the planet. This phase has now been completed by you.

The paramount next step is for you to be able to realign to the sacred that you are in Truth. Through your Home Space you have established a reconnection to the energetic components of your multidimensionality. Through this reconnection you have been energetically prepared and aligned, to be able to assimilate all the Group Mind multidimensional frequencies of light that exists. You can energetically carry the full potential for your self-realization process. You are able to adapt and align to the full potency of your God aspect through the cells of your physical body. You are ready!

This reconnection to your Home Space has birthed new electrical settings through all of your systems to enable you to hold the energetic light frequency of your place within the Collective Group Mind. Through the changes of your own multidimensionality you will begin to open and experience the Knowledge that has existed in a Timeless space within the multidimensional settings of the Collective One. This is one aspect of the Collective Group Mind.

Remember: Your receptor in the brain is connected directly to the Collective Group Mind consciousness. This transmission form can be likened to an umbilical cord. You are being fed a pure frequency of Truth that is held within a container of love from the Collective Group consciousness.

Your new electrical settings within will allow you to hold the full frequencies of the Knowledge as you evolve. This frequency will be embedded through your energetic field and then transmitted into your newly awakened brain receptor. Once it is within the brain there will be a filtering process that activates a birthing of light filaments within the receptor.

The element of God is held within the frequencies that are transmitted to you within your receptor in the brain. Slowly you will absorb this light of God. This needs to be ingested in layers, through each transmitter that already exists within every cell of your body. Through these transmitters the God element will begin to activate a frequency of Truth through your heart, Home Space, and outward to all of humanity who are ready to move into their next phase.

Your reconnection to us, the Group Mind, will open up and expand areas of the brain that hold the electrical components of the frequency of the Knowledge. Once again you will be able to hold the sacred force of the frequency held within the Knowledge. This energy leads you to be able to consciously enter the Time Line space. The Time Line will open a door to a limitless potential, and will carry the multidimensional pure form creation energy.

We all carry the Time Line component within the Group Mind consciousness, and you are a natural extension within this element of connection. The Knowledge that is contained within the sacred texts is woven within the frequency that we collectively hold. The sacred teachings are defined specifically within the collective energy that we anchor within the universal setting.

All Knowledge creates a powerful clarity within, a peaceful sacred setting for rejuvenation and regeneration of the spiritual force of the One. The teachings are contained through the One. This force of love evolves through us, and then outward. The Truth always contains love and remains unchanged through all time. We embrace all that exists with that love.

The Knowledge is where all understanding resides in that timeless state. This place holds the sacred Truth of all dimensional levels for all time and carries the sacred texts and laws of light that are made manifest throughout the Universes. The Knowledge holds the unlimited frequencies of the sacred realms of the God consciousness and Godhead energy that contains the full creation light. This Knowledge gives you access to the multidimensional currents that exist and have been housed within the Universes for the sole purpose of creation. The Knowledge holds the full creation elements that have been the foundation for the sacred moments within the fulfillment of all the self-realized prophecies.

Through the Knowledge you are brought back to the sacredness of life after lying dormant forever. We likened it to springtime after an endless cold winter. You begin to radiate and blossom as a new shoot on a branch of a tree emerging. These shoots are your innate aspect of God, of the One. Each of you carries this original Imprint form that holds the completed frequency of God. Each individual fragment of the frequency holds this aspect of the One. This is the God element that holds the purest light consciousness that contributes to the Collective Group Mind dynamic.

The Hologram that is anchored through the Covenant supports the Platform for the full frequency of Knowledge to be anchored and then to be imparted to all who are ready. These elements carry the natural action of love. They have been made manifest through contributing to this awakening force. This activation of the Knowledge that is aligned within you opens up a compelling need for you to move with a sacred timing of divine proportions. You enter the holy realms through the Knowledge and you are initiated to hold the sacred within you. This sacred aspect moves through you with impeccable timing, your actions carry the authority of the One.

This whole process of returning needs to be a conscious action by you. This is imperative for the completion phase of your role within the New Dawning prophecy. There is a need for you to understand what is before you, what is within you, what your next stage of unfolding requires of you. We hold the One within us, the Collective Group Mind. You are an aspect of the One. This is Truth.

Now it is your time to anchor through your Home Space and begin your conscious realignments. Your Home Space is your connecting rod for your conscious re-emergence to the Group Mind Consciousness.

The energy of the sacred is woven through the grand design, of which you are a part. In Truth there has not been a moment that you have been separated from these teachings held within this grand design. Your Home Space is your pathway to the reconnection to your Imprint. Your reconnection to the grand design is imbedded within your Imprint. First, you need to reach within your Home Space and align to Self. Remember who you are and what you are in reality. You are working through the command of the awakened aspect of Self. This is who you are, and through this aspect of Self you have already entered a sacred communion with the Collective Group Mind.

A large part of your awakening is to come to a Truth: You have never been separate from this grand plan. You have participated within this plan by being on this earth plane in human form. You have played an integral role of awakening through your human experience and now you are re-emerging through your higher consciousness to your spiritual aspect. Throughout your journey on the earth plane as a human being, you have always been part of the Collective Group Mind, always an aspect of the One. This is Truth.

Come home; come home, Beloved. We await your conscious reconnection!

Blessings,
The Collective Group Mind

Note: You   can   find   an   audio   file   link   at *www.christinedayonline.com/pleiadianpromise*

You can utilize this multidimensional journey often for your ongoing unfolding. Each time you work with these energies you will move to a higher frequency of your own sacred awakening. The sacred sound that is given will resonate and align you within the sacred currents that exist in your place within the Collective Group Mind.

We hold you as you birth.

Collective Group Mind Patterning

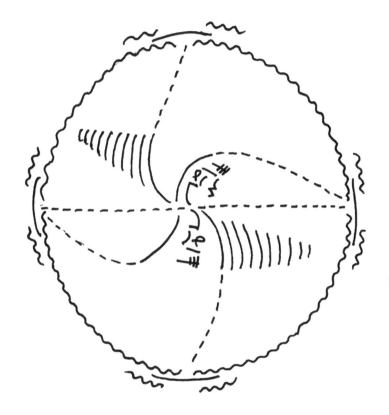

Sound: ALESTAH

CHAPTER 4

WE THE GALACTIC COMMUNITY

As we align to Truth through the Collective Group Mind, we will experience within our heart the purest form of unity. This pure connection within our heart carries the fulfillment of the Promise that exists between human beings and the Galactic Community within this Universe. This is the moment for the Promise to be self-actualized within us. There has been an opening of a fifth and sixth dimensional Time Frame within our planet earth. This access has been expressly established and will continue to be developed for a forging of alliances between those of us on the awakening path and the Galactic Community.

This ongoing change of dimensional dynamics taking place on our planet aids us in forming alliances with those Communities with whom we originated. We as a human race are required to consciously open to a Truth that mirrors this unity. This Truth holds the deep spiritual connecting link that exists with the Galactic Community and humanity. Each one of us individually needs to meet and walk this pathway that has been recently revealed, in order for us to return to the sacred union with our neighbors and family within the Galactic Community.

There is a sacred foundation to be built and laid between us. Then this energy of our collective synergy will to be launched within the Galactic Community and throughout this Universe. This sacred reunion needs to be initiated and developed by those of us who are already aware of the nature of the Galactic groups and the sacred ties that bind us. We are being called forward now, all who are ready to expand these connections to a different dimensional setting. To be willing to open into the various factions within the Galactic Community and allow a steady birthing, a rejoining of consciousness to evolve on yet another level within our Communities. This is a necessary step that will support and accelerate our own Community development on the planet during this next phase of transition.

I am clearly being shown that within our earth plane there are sacred reconnections currently established between all facets of the Galactic Community and certain individual human groups on our planet. This means we are definitely ready to move into this next step as a collectively awakened human group.

The Galactic Community exists within the exact same multidimensional Time Frames within the Universe as we on planet Earth. These Time Frames are designed to link us together within this incarnation and at a certain moment forge our connections through a collective link held by the God Consciousness state. This specific energetic link is designed to bring us together to support each other in the unfolding of our individual and collective transitions.

Understand the Galactic Community as a collective are playing major parts in our transition. They have been holding and continually adjusting the energetic settings that have been playing a significant role in the dimensional adjustments on our planet. They also keep the ancient energies in place so they can be re-established on our earth plane for us to align to our sacred reconnections once again.

At a certain moment we will have a strong role to play for the Galactic Community. This Time Frame link has a unique design to enable mankind to support the Galactic Community in their own evolution within their own societies. This support is designed to take place when we, as humans, begin to shift into our individual enlightenment power and move our consciousness into a sacred communion light with them. Through this unity, we can then enter through the collective communion energy, and interact as fully participating members of this group within the Galactic Community in our Universe.

This communion with humanity is also designed to transform the Galactic Community, enabling them to move into an elevated rhythm of vibrational consciousness through this reconnection with us. This sacred forging will set in motion a predestined event that has been waiting to come to pass within the Galactic Community. They will form a new God state within their own Communities through this re-established link with us on planet Earth.

We, as a human race, need to let go into the current that is now accessible to us and open consciously toward this union. This flow is dynamic in nature and is designed to position us to totally embody this sacred union with the Galactic Community. This stream moves us into a setting that radiates, revealing the completion energy of this full transition that is to take place. The anointing that will occur within the sacred fusion of this communion will be anchored by the Hologram, and held within the Covenant.

This connection will unfold us into our full potential of awakening, fulfilling an aspect of the Prophecy, held by the Covenant. As a human race we open up through our creative frequency, and there is a rebirthing of a raw untapped aliveness that will return through our conscious state as we evolve within this expanding union within the Galactic Community.

The moment has come for the sacred revelations of light to shine forth upon us all, joining us in Community and ending the separation with every faction that makes up the Galactic Community and humanity. This will bring to a close the misunderstandings of the past, which have been created through the misinterpretations held within our third-dimensional illusions and the limitations we have, until recently, been operating within on our planet.

Barriers of fear and confusion have built up over a series of lifetimes. These have opened deep wounds within some of us on Earth. There have been stories about abductions. Yet many of these proclaimed abductions have been pre-agreements that were being fulfilled, made by individuals who as part of their natural heritage have an alien element within them. Their alien experience played an essential role in the destiny of their awakening, regardless of their ego minds' misperception and assessment of their process as being a victim.

There have been some exceptions with abductions by the Greys in the past. Know that there have been formidable interventions by the Galactic Council, whose role is to oversee and monitor the entire Universe. These abductions by the Greys have been stopped.

The Galactic Council currently oversees our individual transition taking place within our physical systems and are currently supervising many of the energetics that are being birthed on our planet. The Ashtar Command is a division of the Galactic Council, which is part of this Federation. These members' sole mission is dedicated to helping us in our ascension process.

There has been a huge gap between the Truth that has been held between our own sacred connections to our Galactic family and the thought processes, the misperceptions held within humankind's ego mind. The Galactic Community has always been perceived as some sort of threat because they live beyond the earth plane, out in an unknown region, portrayed as dangerous and misunderstood. There has been a lot of terror perpetuated around the alien energies, through stories about imminent invasions of our Earth by extraterrestrial forces.

Some of the Galactic races have a very different physical appearance, more along the lines of reptilian. This abnormality in appearance also feeds into the fear. Whenever there is talk of Aliens, fear has always been a strong knee-jerk reaction with the ego mind, and this fear is perpetuated by the third-dimensional illusion that humans are the only existing race.

This insight of our extended family begins to lead us into fulfilling an aspect of a collective mission with the Galactic Community. Our individual understanding of Truth accesses the frequency of the sacred design alignment to "coming home." We come Home to ourselves through the acceptance of our place within this Galactic Community reconnection. We are shifted dimensionally to meet the higher potential of ourselves.

Just our intention alone to move our awareness toward the Galactic Community is potent, and opens us up into the sacred link that has always existed between us. This impacts the sacred design originally formed and held within the Covenant for us to align. We are creators, and through our thought patterns we can create a changing element of bridging within this new dynamic.

There are many diverse Galactic groups that make up the full Galactic Community. We each resonate with some groups more than others, because of our heritage or through pre-agreements. These alliances are imperative to the big picture and we can trust the depth of these heart connections. Now we will find an acceleration take place with these communion relationships. Through these connections, essential building blocks will be established for the ultimate union of our collective Communities.

In our ongoing birthing process with the Galactic Community we will glimpse ourselves in a new light, with the growing awareness of who we are in reality, and coming into an understanding of the profound role that we are to play within the Galactic Community. The Truth is: We are all an interwoven aspect of the God Consciousness. We are not separate from each other. We have an unfolding history together that is a collective part of us.

There will be an unveiling of sacred revelations of the individual roles that we are to play collectively within the next step of awakening in the Universe. This process of reconnection to our place within the Galactic Community will bring to us, and to the earth plane, a new level of maturity in relationship with the Universe. As we learn to reach out through our spiritual alignments and activate our potential through this sacred alliance with the Galactic Community, we will flourish in dynamic new ways.

Some of us, as part of our mission here on the earth plane, are to play a prominent role in this re-emergence of communion with the Galactic Community at this juncture. We are to hold the energetic Imprint Platform for all of humanity. In Truth, none of us who have incarnated on the earth plane is originally from Earth.

There are the Starseeds that play an essential part on our planet Earth. They hold an essence for us to awaken. They originate from various worlds within the Galactic Federation. They have a regular form as a human, who have taken birth just like everyone else, however, their spiritual lineage is not native to this world. These people carry and transmit a pure form of love, holding a mirror for us to be able to open into a conscious-ness of love that we have the potential to embody. They also bring to us a deep awareness of the significance of our place on the earth plane and our place that exists in the Universe. They are channels for information and bring clarity to support us in our journey homeward. This awakening they bring to us has been preordained as part of the New Dawning grand plan for humanity and for the planet to fully align back to the Galactic Community.

There are children coming in, known as Indigos and Crystal children, who are born in bodies more highly evolved than most humans. They are all carrying the energies of this awakening process within them. They are holding a mirrored energy and naturally transmitting outward this expand-ing light frequency that supports the transition of the planet. By maintaining strong alignments to their unique origins within the Galactic Community, their energies are an anchor for humanity and the Earth's transformation.

These lineages reside within individuals who carry a specific mission for the planet. They have come to bring us support in our awakening here on the earth plane and our reconnections to the Galactic Community. Through these individuals we are able to alter our perception and begin to open into a deepening awareness of the existence of an extraterrestrial presence. We have all come here to have a full human experience, and yet we carry a native heritage aspect within us, originating from Galactic Universal roots.

The Galactic Federation is a large federation, and they have witnessed the civilization of many different planets, Star Systems within Galaxies, and Universes. Through the Collective Group Mind they are able to work together for the harmonious existence of all life. The Galactic Federation holds a place of consciousness in each of the inhabited galaxies of our Universe. This is part of the universal management structure devoted to universal peace and harmony. This Galactic Federation of Light is com-posed of many different life force groups, from many worlds committed to the cause of helping Earth ascend.

There are those from the Galactic Community who are coming to our planet, from the other civilizations within the Galaxy, working to-gether to change the energetic dimensional states as we are being stabi-lized through the Hologram held within the Covenant. We all hold the

God Consciousness aspect within us and we are interconnected through the Collective Group Mind to all life force in the Universe. The birthing of a new conscious world will herald in our homecoming on planet Earth. We will return Home to rejoin the rest of the Collective Universal Community through this higher consciousness state.

There are many human beings on the planet who are affiliated with different life force groups. They have been aligning energetically, and working tirelessly on various projects to prepare our Earth for this next phase. They have been forming a union through a combined consciousness with all teams to support the anchoring of a new light cycle on our planet. Collectively they are activating Portals, anchoring grid lines, aligning closely through a new Time Frame frequency in readiness for the birthing of this new energetic Community Base to be established within the Core of our planet.

We begin a powerful turning point in the history of the Earth. This will be a profound, life-altering time for humankind. We are being called to activate and begin a unique birthing process, through receiving that which has always been sacred within the Universe. Most importantly this is a fundamental part of our divine heritage. This sacredness is held in the form of an energetic Base.

The Base holds a Blueprint that carries sacred texts, releases information, understanding, and brings clarity to the full Community here on Earth. Through a natural absorption process we are enabled to set in motion and activate a profound transforming element within the consciousness of our society. These sacred texts bring the frequency to develop a new conscious state within us individually. The anchoring of this Base is imperative to the success of manifesting a transformed framework of a collective society on Earth in this New Dawning era.

Through a conscious reconnection, by those of us who have been on the path of awakening, we will be able to develop and activate this Base through our collective consciousness. This is the only option available, because we must birth this Base by ourselves as a collective human entity. Yes, there will be support given within the process by the Galactic Community; however, we must take ownership of this birthing process as human beings. This is an essential requirement for our own evolution on Earth.

This has always been the plan: the development of our own conscious society through the utilization of a master light Blueprint held within the Base. The Blueprint carries multidimensional patterns that we will manifest from, once the Core is anchored and established on the Earth. This patterning design will hold our own unique Community frequency, a sacred design that creates pure forms of consciousness that cradles us as a collective group. This will activate a transmission, moving outward carrying the Truth of our very existence that is to come. Through this Truth an Overlay will be made from the God Consciousness that will flow throughout our planet, forging a new paradigm within our newly formed Communities.

This sacred Overlay that forms from the patterning will exist at the very center of each collective Community. It will anchor and operate through the central Core within the planet. This Overlay will dramatically affect the energetic dynamic played out by humanity, revealing a sacred space held within the earth plane. This will accelerate the potential for all who reside on the Earth by opening up and unveiling a sacred aspect of our consciousness within this new era of light. This is the dynamic that has been pre-ordained to take place and will allow us to move into our expanded potential within the entire Universe through a collective communion.

This transitional phase will herald in the state of consciously Being. This will be the sacred manifestation created within all life force energy of the planet. The Overlay is an unending, evolutionary process that opens the unlimited potential of the God element to manifest within our Communities.

This pure form of God that births through the Overlay from the Base is uniquely designed for Community on Earth, opening up a framework for all of us within our society to thrive with our own individuality within our spiritual natures. This allows each one of us to become "the gift" to the new Community frequency, and we achieve this through Being. Through this full expression of our consciousness we will be able to support each other to move naturally back into the full alliance with the Universal energy. We return as a Community to the One. Our patterning will be able to birth naturally through the universal flow bringing completion. We each get to choose the moment to move back into this alignment.

Many of the Galactic Community are waiting for those of us who are ready to begin this next part of the project.

A Message From the Galactic Community

Beloved ones, we greet you.

We are the One; you are the One. We support the unfolding of these new understandings of your time. We hold the studies of the light within our hearts for you. We carry all that you need in the way of support for the building of your own community light. We bring the knowledge of Community to you through our own direct experience through the One. We bring the higher knowledge that has been anchored through our own Communities for your individual process of unfolding within your own. This holding by us is energetic, and will enable you to begin to weave a cycled structure of light for your unique Community Base form consciousness. You do not need to begin from a starting point, rather come from our Base that has been formed through the ancient texts and that has been in place operating for eons within our own Communities.

Our Base was forged through the God energy at the same moment that you were first conceived within the Collective Group Mind. This sacred cycle that emerges from the Base embodies the God frequency of love. This fluid cycle contained within the Base was an original design for our Community and opens a framework for all within our society to thrive within their own uniqueness.

This is the time for you to move, finding a new regime, a new frequency to anchor within your own society. We hold the frequency of the full Base framework steady for you. The timing is right to begin opening up to this project of anchoring the sacred cycle Base between the many groups that are already formed between you on your earth plane.

Many of you hold this designed process within, and are now ready to anchor this Base. This has been pre-ordained as part of your mission. This sacred happening that is held within your mission energy contributes to you being able to birth your cycle Base for the Earth through your individual groups. As you begin to draw from the energy of this Base an aspect of this self-realization path is completed. Each one of you, regardless of whether you hold this design process, will be able to have a strong impact on the development of your cycle Base for your planet. Every human being holds within them the potential to play their unique role in the development of the Base for the planet.

All you need in the moment is a willingness to open and receive the sacred teachings that exist with this Truth, which is contributing to the purpose of these sacred activations. Honor your place here on the earth plane. Honor each other and the individual roles that you play, one is not more than another. Now is time to anchor this holy form, of the cycle Base within your Earth's Core.

As you begin to activate the Base there will be a multilayered opening formed, holding the ancient imprints. It will contain an intricate frequency that will be dimensionally layered through the limitless space within the Core of the Earth. As a group, you will collectively witness the birth of this profound frequency as the full Base anchors within the Core. With the completion of the anchoring of your Base, you will experience a weaving and connecting link unfolding within your own heart space. You will each hold a component of the sacred communion of Community within.

To begin to work through the Base energy, you will be moved into the limitless fluidity of the Core in a joint communion of consciousness through your combined synergy. Your own awareness will be able to expand naturally through the pure form held through your collective group communion. This will present as a timeless energy connection to the Core, enveloping the full group consciousness, and birthing the group's dynamic potential.

Once the Base energy is anchored through the Core of the Earth, the next step is the birthing of Earth's sacred design, which will hold the holy substance from which your Community will arise. As this sacred cycle completes itself there will be the birth of the pure Hologram formed by the Base. This Hologram will contain the sacred design of the Community and this patterning will hold the mirror of the completed aspect of your individual Community light.

We bring the wisdom of our experience and impart this to you. This is our sacred role that we have been given. A sacred trust handed to us by

God. This is a mission that touches the deepest aspect of our own sacred nature. We are the One; you are the One.

There is no difference between you and us, when we are all anchored within the Higher Realms. We merge through the Collective Group Mind. We meet as One with you. We are to work together as one consciousness; that is the grand plan. As the One we are in perfect alignment. We call to you now to open into this understanding, into the moment of Truth, and through this Truth we reconnect with you.

Know that we can only bring this support by being summoned by you. We cannot invade your space with the information, or bring the details of the change to you without your permission, without your heartfelt call. Remember this: We, our hearts, your hearts are interconnected through that Collective Group Mind, and in reality nothing will ever change this Truth.

There is much to be achieved on your planet to get ready for this sacred integration. There is a necessary process of lining up a series of energetic forms on your planet for this next step. This involves a series of dimensional shifts opening along selected grid lines throughout your earth plane. We are to play a further role through the supervision of these alignments, working alongside you. With many of our groups working beside you, the time for this renewal is close.

Through this preparation a deepening of our communion energy will be re-established. This will re-open between us the sacred resolution of Truth, revealing a fuller aspect of the plan. We hold the full synergistic profiles of this time ahead within us.

You hold within you the sacred Time Lines from which you can draw. As you birth your Base Communities on your planet you will naturally reconnect into these Time Lines. These Time Lines hold a steady vibration around the entire transitional phase and the outcome is assured.

Now is the time for the Master Game to begin through this resurrection of our sacred alliance.

Blessings,

Through the Pleiadians, from the Galactic Community

Through our collective awakened state as human beings, we can move beyond the veils into this expanded dimensional communion state. As a collective group we, as humans, can begin to build a powerful state of one consciousness collectively. We will then align to the sacred understandings of our unlimited abilities within that collective power. Through our awakening process we will enter a new state of Being, balancing in the Higher Realms and interacting with the individual factions of the Galactic Community within their own settings.

Rarely has it been written in the history of planet Earth for any one of us as humans to be able to touch or impact the Galactic Community in any positive, supportive way. Now we will take our rightful place within the Universe, within the Galactic Communities, as we fulfill our awakening role. There are many details to come, however, right now the message is the message. All we need to understand is the existence of our sacred connection to the Galactic Community realms, and through this unveiling there is the vast potential that is to come through the forging of our relationship with them.

Acknowledging this Truth sets in motion a connection to the energetic Blueprint held by the Covenant, which is to unfold. There will be a sacred fusion with the Galactic Community as we fulfill our own awakening role through the birthing of our Base and community frequency design.

As this sacred connection to the Galactic Community takes place there is a metamorphic change that will expand through our heart cells. The transformer within our cells will open up a new setting place that will expand a telepathic connection from within our heart cells to the receptor in the brain. This revolutionary process will allow a heightened level of communion to be made possible, which will open up expanded lines of communication to the Galactic Community, supporting our reunion.

We will be interconnected neighbors joined through a sacred consciousness communion. This is the time for the gap between the Galactic Community and us to begin to transform, re-establishing that which we are a part of, the holy connection.

This sacred resolution is coming, and is made possible through the New Dawning energy that impacts all of us within this Galaxy and the entire Universe. All life forces are being compelled to move forward now, especially those of us who are predestined to be leaders in this process. We "way showers" on Earth are to forge the path.

As we individually allow our inner transformations and realign consciously through the Group Mind, enlightenment will be made manifest. As a human race, through our creation element, a series of dimensional shifts, like waves rolling across the Galaxy, will reform the entire sacred patterning held within the Universe. This unfolding will create a complete and new potential for all life force energies within the collective energies.

There is a fluid light shield, likened to a womb around our earth plane, while we move through this very dynamic and profound awakening. This is necessary while we transition and stabilize within our new Community Base. We are held as we complete the forming of this strong and holy coalition with the rest of the Galactic Community within the Universe.

Many of us have been connecting strongly to different factions of the Galactic Community. We are the "way showers" in this project and so the door opens first to those of us who are already in direct contact with the Galactic Community. Through this doorway there is a call going out. This call is for us to begin a new conscious alignment through building an expanded connection with others on the same path, building a consolidated Community.

There is a great need for this opening of Community between us, which is achieved by initially developing a strong form of telepathic communion between our individual group, and then reaching out to other formed groups.

We need to work through the format that is given to us by the Galactic Community, utilizing the Base form and anchoring it through the Core of the Earth, then manifesting our unique design patterning through the Base that will birth the individual group's new Community Design.

Each one of us is being called now. This is a pre-destined, pre-agreement for many of us. I personally hold a space and the Platform for this aspect of the mission to be actualized.

1. Birth the Base Core Energy of Earth—Sound: CRESTAH EE...
2. Birth the Community Patterning Design—Sound: KAYSTAH

Note: You   can   find   two   audio   files   at *www.christinedayonline.com/pleiadianpromise*

You will work with the Blueprint Patterning Circle design (see the diagram on page 89) in conjunction with both audio files.

1ST STAGE: The audio file will align you and your group to the Galactic Base, and then take you in a step-by-step process to anchor the Galactic Base through the Core of the Earth. This anchoring of the Base within the Core of the Earth will be done in layers, dimensional phases. Just let go and move with the transmissions contained within the Audio file. Remember as you engage through the Base you will go through powerful initiations within your heart cells. As you bring your awareness into this design you will be given access to the Base energy. You will utilize a sacred sound to align deeper within the Base energy to begin to anchor this Base through the Earth's core.

2ND STAGE: You will begin to activate the patterning of our new community on the earth plane through the blueprint held within the Base. Remember, this Blueprint births the sacred patterning for Community on planet Earth. This patterning will hold the frequency to transform the Community of the planet.

NOTE: You will use the first sacred sound. As you bring your awareness into the sacred design and use the sacred sound that is given, you will access the Blueprint held within the Base to anchor through the core of the Earth.

You will use the second sacred sound to begin to birth the individual community patterning for the Earth. Know as you work within the developing patterning that you will go through a metamorphic process within you. It is essential to work with others (at least three other people). This is specifically to be activated within a group process.

Blueprint Patterning

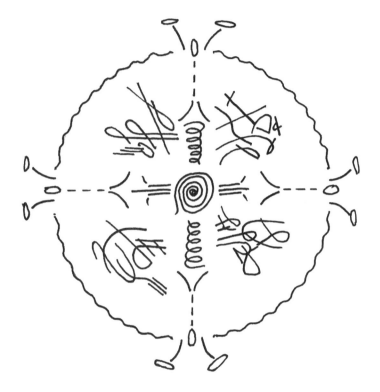

Sound: CRESTAH EE...
Sound: KAYSTAH

Chapter 5

Moving Into New Terrain

Through this sacred time of transition, we have brought ourselves to a transformed place of awareness within, by navigating our own unique pathway of inner development. We have taken many challenging steps forward to move beyond illusion and align to Self. We have answered the call with a strong resolve, moving with the destiny signature within our hearts. This calling has unearthed a strong inner desire to find our own sacredness that resides within the Higher Realms. This path we have forged for ourselves has taken great courage and we have pushed past the illusions of limitation and the attachment of the ego mind to take our rightful place.

There is a destined group forming now of which each one of us is a part, and we each bring our individual unique element to the whole. We are all aligned energetically to make a collective group of "way showers." Our role is to support humanity through the different stages of transition on our Earth. There is a witnessing and acknowledgment of our inner strength and dedication to fulfilling our destiny path.

We, as a human race, have come to planet Earth to have a human experience initially, and then to awaken, fully embracing our sacredness in this lifetime. There are many scenarios within our life experiences that have prepared us to move through to a place of change and into an unfolding of Self. We have been the creator of all of these collective experiences that have brought us to this juncture.

We began our journey being anchored and deeply immersed in a state of separation from our Higher Self energy in the third-dimensional illusion that has existed. Through this separation we have been engulfed within a complete experience of illusion, sometimes playing out a full victim role through the choices that we have made. We have opened ourselves to have a series of direct experiences that we needed in order to move through a series of specific learning processes.

Being in life we learn about our own vulnerabilities and idiosyncrasies as human beings, and get to experience moving through the processes created by our own ego mind judgments. The ego mind fully participates within the illusion. By interacting within the ego we move ourselves into states of suffering and separation that we have manufactured to experience. Within this play out of this illusion has been the perfect orchestration of events created by us, just for ourselves. These events enabled us to have a deep inner process of these third-dimensional experiences, of limitation and separation in our lives.

Each of us is like an actor on a stage. Each one of us has had the lead role in our own play, and we have chosen the actors that accompany us on our stage. Each person we have chosen carries a mirror of what we already have inside of ourselves. They play their role perfectly, acting out, mirroring the limitations or feelings that we have within us. We have had to move through a series of different scenes with each person on that stage. This is one aspect of our creation, our story. We receive the gifts, the teaching that exists within our own unique play that comes from our individual experiences. There have been no wrong choices, no wrong decisions made—just a series of experiences in order for us to learn. We chose all the facets of the play-outs. We got to choose to move into all the dramas of our full creation.

You may want to look at your grand creation that you are living out in your lives now. Everything in your lives arises from within us. Life holds the full reflection of what is already in existence within us, unexpressed. We are truly the creator at the center of our Universe.

A key element on this journey of separation is suffering. Suffering arises through the deeply, sometimes hidden belief that we do not deserve the love. We do not deserve to receive the abundance. Suffering arises from a misinterpretation and misperception of our ego mind about our self, and who we are within our life. The ego mind only sources from past experiences, taking on judgments from our parents and society, and holding onto the limited belief systems. We often begin to take on the judgmental role of others by condemning ourselves, creating an internal war that opens through us, creating a deep, internal separation.

Suffering is not a necessity for living. Suffering is largely an aspect of the illusion, connected to the past and to those old belief systems held within the ego mind. We can actually choose to let go of suffering at any moment. Many of us have been programmed that we somehow deserve to suffer—that suffering is a requirement to live.

The ego mind constantly needs to understand what is going on by assessing us, and everything around us. The ego mind is addicted to trying to understand, to stay in control. The ego mind's need to understand actually stops us from letting go and just being in our experience fully. If we begin to let go of the need to understand and the need to be right, we will start to let go of the suffering, and begin to set ourselves free. The need to understand is totally overrated and unnecessary. The ego mind is the only aspect of us that needs to understand. This letting go is an essential ingredient to self-liberation and leads us back to a self-loving state. We need to give ourselves permission to let go now!

One aspect of our journey on this Earth was to have this human experience within the illusion, to be in a completely disconnected state from our sacred nature. Then at some moment, the veils would lift like a curtain on a stage, and we would begin to awaken as we moved beyond the illusion. We could start to glimpse our sacredness and embark on a conscious reconnection to this new path of awakening. Simultaneously, we would be building a bridge between the spiritual and human aspect of our selves, forming a new dynamic with our humanness.

The earth plane has already begun to shift from its original purpose of anchoring the third-dimensional illusion in place. This strong foundation of separation is crumbling with these changes. We are now completing this first phase of our journey of limitation. Through this new role that the Earth is playing, there has been a series of newly anchored multidimensional doorways that have created a profound opening for those of us who are ready for this next phase of transitioning. We are entering this next step of experiencing the awakening of our own consciousness, reopening into our sacred natures. We who are the "way showers" are to play an essential role on planet Earth and within the Universe. In this transitional phase on Earth we re-emerge into our spiritual natures, beginning to see, sense, and directly experience a shifting process within our journey as our limitations melt away.

Our reason for being on this planet is rapidly changing. We are emerging through this interconnection into our own spiritual nature. We will be transformed through these new multidimensional settings of light that are unveiling, giving us access to the Higher Realm connections of Self. Through this metamorphic process on Earth many of us are beginning to remember and fully connect with who we are, and to comprehend the fuller roles that we are meant to play, and participate through our newly birthed consciousness. We are being asked to foster sacred relationships within this new energetic setting that contains this Higher Realm consciousness.

We have many life force groups within the Galactic Community and the entire Universes supporting us in this next transitional phase of our awakening. At this juncture it is essential for us to consciously develop and build these alliances. This next phase is going to be a rapid process that will propel each of us who are ready into a completely different dimensional realm.

There will continue to be discrepancies because of the multidimensional realities that will still exist on Earth. We can expect these different realities between communities to continue for some time. There are many multidimensional realities playing out on Earth simultaneously; this has always been. During this transitional phase, there will be even broader dimensional gaps with individual experiences on the planet.

There is a variation of dimensional setting experiences between those who are waking up quickly and those who are still caught up in the separation of illusion. There are those who are in violent realities and immersed in deep power struggles. Know how essential it is to allow others to have the experiences they need for their full expression. We need to give them the respect of being where they are and living in their own creation. These individuals do not need to be saved. They are having their own experiences. This process applies to all of us. Wherever each of us is in our lives right now, we must embrace our experience and honor our own creation.

Those of us who are the "way showers" will exist in one reality while others on the planet will still be playing out the illusion and in another reality. Again, it is essential that we do not try to fix these discrepancies within individuals, but continue to allow each individual to play out their own reality to its completion. Our role is to hold the energy around the entire outcome for the Earth, which will come to pass. This is assured. This split will not last forever, and is only a temporary state, a necessary process for a successful completion of Earth's transition.

During this unfolding process the "way showers" stabilize the energetic frequency on the planet. So this next step of the transition depends on us, as the first group leading the way by holding an energetic setting for the entire Community on the planet. Each one of us has been walking our path to prepare ourselves for this event. An energetic womb will be established in readiness for the birthing of the masses within this new Community design. Each individual will be received through an aspect of their light consciousness that will be contained within this womb as part of their destiny. They will awaken and remember their sacredness at a certain moment. This is the way the process of our new Community is to be completed.

We, as human beings, have spent lifetimes playing in this field of the third-dimensional illusion on our planet. All of us who are here at this time have said "yes" to being here now. It is considered a great privilege to be here during this transitional process at this sacred time on Earth, to play our individual and collective roles in this whole unfolding process.

This is a rare, sacred time in the history of the earth plane. Never before has there been the potential for this level of awakening that is about to unfold. We have all been handpicked to join together in this extraordinary setting and to participate in birthing a glorious Community together. This Community will impact the entire consciousness within our Universe and the Collective Universes.

We individually get to be a catalyst for transforming the Earth. We get to rise like a glorious Sun, with the flowing light rays moving outwards to touch all life force on this planet and then extending those light rays outwards within the Universe. We become the light, the New Dawning consciousness that has been promised. We become that light and arrive Home. We will hold the full frequency of this light alive within us.

We, as a group, are now ready for this transitional phase to begin within us. We are being moved into a deep initiation process, to what is known as an Awakening Frequency Pulse that will bring us into an alignment within a sacred state, enabling us to fully function in our upcoming roles.

This Pulse is a dimensional frequency of pure love that will be unknown, unrecognizable to us from an ego mind perspective. The ego mind will not be able to understand, interpret, or make sense of its purpose. Most significantly the ego mind will not be able to interfere with this unfolding. This process is natural to your spiritual nature. This is a perfectly designed orchestration for us to fulfill the Promise.

The timing for this transitional phase is to begin, at a precisely lined-up moment, through the Prophecies that have been written. There is a sacred alignment, a signature in place within the star systems to herald this happening. This signature place is here to support the expansive energy that will be generated by what is referred to as the Awakening Frequency Pulse. This star system carries the energetic design to hold an anchor in place and forge the brilliant light of a new consciousness that will be generated through the activation of this Frequency Pulse. This Awakened Frequency Pulse is part of the Promise energy that the Pleiadians are revealing to all of us who are ready.

These phrases that are contained within this Frequency Pulse open up a sacred awakening within us. They carry all the dimensional settings of Truth. The words collectively create the Awakening Frequency Pulse, and they contain the full frequencies for this next phase of our unfolding—of our birth. They carry the potential form of the expanded element of our sacred energy that exists on this new path that we are destined to begin. This path will move us to a state of vision in which we will receive the clarity to transform consciously. As we are given new revelations, new understandings of Self, we will effortlessly reconnect to an aspect of our authenticity. Our awareness will be moved to fully align to all that is Truth within. There is no halfway point of measure within this process. We are to simply realign to that which is the holy, authentic aspect of Self.

This sacred weaving of our Self has been preordained to exist within us. This sacredness is to be woven through all of humanity and outward, naturally flowing into the Universal Realms. This unique weaving of ours is to play an essential role as part of the new Community consciousness on Earth. For all of us who are awake, it is time to begin to allow this free-flowing sacred weave of ourselves to be realized. We have nothing to hide, nothing to be fearful about as we return to our full fluid state. We need to let go and allow this new uninhibited flow to be an innate aspect of our human physical body.

The vibrational level of the physical body will transform; the cells within the body will become fluid as we birth this brilliant light within us. As we take the Promise energy through the words of the Awakening Frequency Phase we will become all that multidimensional brilliance, an indescribable form that is held within the powerful authenticity of Self.

There will be a seamless movement of fluidity, carrying this brilliance being absorbed through the physical vehicle as our cells transform. As we let go and allow this depth of unfolding to unravel within us there will be an adjustment period. This journey of working within the Awakening Frequency Phrases is designed to take us one step at a time, so there will be a gradual, dynamic unfolding within this brilliance of Self. We will embark on a new learning curve of navigating ourselves differently in this world, acclimating to a new fluid state of being as part of our natural makeup.

Remember: This whole process is our Spiritual aspect birthing us—a sacred happening that has been preordained and pre-agreed by us, to take place on Earth. Many of us have chosen to take this step now, and this will be a unique and collective experience for all.

This process is essential to your unfolding. You will open into the experience of this sacred text and begin to receive the living vibrations that exist within the frequency created, formed by the words.

Do not stop reading the full text of the Awakening Frequency Pulse until you have read all that is written on the page. You must always read the complete form—every word.

Allow a weaving of these energies from the words to move through you. Each time you take in these frequencies, by reading the full phrases on the page, you will realign to that which is sacred within you on a multidimensional level. These frequencies contained within the words come from the Higher Realm consciousness setting. They are held within a sacred, Timeless space.

This is your moment for the full phrase of the words to become manifest within you. You do not need to comprehend what the words are saying to you; simply reading them and then letting go is enough. Each time you open to a new level of these frequencies held by the phrases you open into the energetic expression of completion elements of Self. This will activate a profound birthing process within. Through your transformation you become a catalyst of being able to hold the glorious light form of the New Dawning energy within you. (See the diagram on page 103.)

"You Are Who You Have Been Waiting For"

Go to the end of this chapter to work with the Awakening Frequency Pulse process. Do this now, before you continue with this chapter. Read the words regularly, allowing the birthing process to complete itself within you. There are dimensional layers to be birthed; just let go and don't monitor your experience.

We have each come here in this incarnation to fulfill our full role of awakening. Through our collective transformation we will begin to development our new Community on Earth. We have several Masters working directly with us during this transitional phase. We have the pure energy of the Christ bringing the sacred Imprints of our multidimensional resurrection as we move through the different layers of our awakening. We are to work alongside the Pleiadians, the Christ energy, and Mother Mary, who will be dedicated to supporting all life force on planet Earth during this dynamic transition as we initiate through this Awakening Frequency.

The Christ energy will enter a new energetic profile with those of us who are open to receiving the sacred Christ purpose in the form of his delivery light. This specific light is held within a sacred ancient realm that has been woven through the Christ ministry from the Timeless space. This light has the characteristic of a flaming torch that holds a quickening, likened to fire. This purity contained within the flame holds the consciousness that carries a signature of the "completion life force" of us, of all humanity, and our full Community frequency design. This signature of the completed life force that we are is the combined light communion of all our souls.

Mother Mary plays a profound role for each of us as she radiates out the pure frequency of the Mother. Through her natural state of being she unfolds the heart, infusing the heart with the holy vibration of light. She presents through this transmission the pure frequencies that are required for us to fully thrive in our new Community on Earth. The infusion of her holy vibration will bring a deep metamorphosis into the vessel of the heart, opening up a complete expanded framework. This birthing of the sacred heart opens a transmutation at the very center of the heart, enabling new levels of compassion and love to permeate through humankind. The sacred heart will complete this transition within our new Community design.

This transmutation of our heart is part of our natural destiny to open into a new state of receivership in our lives. This process within the heart is an opportunity for us to begin a new relationship with Self. We will then be able to receive our self on another dimensional level of love, being complete within ourselves to hold the love and compassion within us. This new vibration of love will transform the energy on Earth, through our holding this self-loving element. Love is the transforming element for humankind.

Mother Mary holds the full reflections of the sacred heart energy in alignment with Christ. Between them they carry aspects of the Promise energy that is aligned through by the Pleiadian consciousness. As you work within the Awakening Frequencies you begin to enter into a new level of relationship with these Master energies.

There is a profound initiation being extended to you with a Sacred Chalice, which is held by Mother Mary. Through all time this Chalice has been accessible for all life force groups within the Universe as they are ready. This is the first time it has been offered to humankind.

The sacred is unfolding for all of us on planet Earth. There is empowerment offered through the sacred anointing that exists within the Chalice. This is our time to step forward, to be in a state of full receivership as we open up to all that awaits us within the initiation of the Chalice. This receivership is bound through our own sacred nature, and allows the sacred within us to begin to flow and flourish. The Self is able to fully express through a multidimensional level within the heart. We then become our sacred heart.

Through the Chalice initiation you will find a form of fluidity that will support you in letting go of the old, and moving into an embrace of a newness of Self. This process will be simple, an effortless birth.

Mother Mary holds the sacred energies of the Chalice for us until we are ready to claim our own awakening, in a full and glorious completed state. The Chalice holds the full potential of our Community design, containing everything of the new and nothing of the old. It works in alignment with the Christ design light, the pure flame of initiation—carrying the brilliance of this New Dawning time within. It holds steady a framework of this pure design of our Community allowing us to come home to ourselves, aligning all humanity.

The Chalice produces the love that is to be absorbed within our physical framework within our cells. As we move through the different stages of transforming into Self, we will be held within this pure initiating energy supported by Mother Mary. This Chalice holds the multidimensional Blueprints that each one of us requires to operate within the opening of specific Time Frames. Each individual Timeframe exists at different stages of our path within the new Community design phases. We all have unique Blueprint designs that mirror our own paths of destiny throughout this New Dawning era. Remember: You cannot exist on the earth plane without an active Blueprint.

As the individual Blueprint energies from the Chalice are activated, they are woven through your Blueprint that is currently active for this lifetime. The role of this initiating Blueprint is to assist you to be able to transition to a new frequency of awakening that is held within the specific multidimensional Time Frame in which we exist within the moment.

We need to be held by Mother Mary as this new frequency Blueprint is being uniquely designed and woven through us during this full birthing initiation. The light frequency of this Blueprint allows us to move laterally through all dimensional Time Lines, giving us an added ability to travel and transform the denser areas of our earth plane as necessary, and at will, when the timing is right.

Our unfolding process of the sacred will allow us to move into the reflected creation light that exists within the Higher Realms of consciousness. There will be an access point opened up in the right moment that holds the sacred deed for the communion energy that is being held for our newly birthed community here on Earth.

As our Blueprint is released through the Chalice we will be aligned to Mother Mary. She will hold our light frequency to her, and a deep initiation of our heart will begin to evolve through us. This profound initiation energy will hold a pure form of love that will impact our heart cells. This action will birth compassion and activate a self-loving principle within us. This evolutionary frequency of transformative love will support us, and will enable us to play a more complete role in the transitioning of our Earth.

We will be handed back our rightful authority that has been held within our enlightenment profile. This will enable us to resurrect the earth planes energetic settings for a successful completion phase. Receiving back our authority gives us access to our individual enlightenment Knowledge, and this profound source energy will play a key role in our new Community foundation. A joint communion of our enlightenment energies brings a sacred establishment to the Earth; this will complete this second phase.

Through our own transformation and the communion group enlightenment, this unfolding process will be able to birth more levels of multidimensional aspects of this patterning design for Community on Earth to be made manifest. The very essence of this design can be more fully realized and held between us. We hold the sacred future of Earth between our collective communion energy within our Community. We will be instrumental in forging that which is preordained within the scriptures of this New Dawning era.

Awakening Frequency Pulse

You can read it through within your mind or out loud; it does not matter. When you have completed the reading, you need to take a Conscious Breath and just let go. Always use the Conscious Breath each time you complete the reading of the words. Close your eyes and sit quietly. Use the Conscious Breath and let go. Open your awareness into your experience and allow a "settling" within you.

Note: The Conscious Breath is a deep breath in through the mouth, and then a breath out through the mouth. The Conscious Breath says, "Yes, I am willing to let go" and "Yes, I am willing to receive my light."

The Pleiadians hold you and witness you as you take this next step.

Note: You can find an audio file link at *www.christinedayonline.com/pleiadianpromise* This audio will align you to Mother Mary and activate your initiation through the Chalice.

1. Your Awakening Frequency Pulse (page 103)

2. Your Chalice Activation | Sound: DAHST EE... (page 104)

'AWAKENING FREQUENCY PULSE'

Becoming authentically you is the end of one part of your journey that leads you into the destiny of a Timeless new journey.

'**I AM**' carries the aspect of Truth. Through this statement, you are aligned to where you are going, and you find yourself being moved by your higher consciousness into what you have become.

'**I AM**' carries the stillness and moves you to the insight that holds Truth.

At that very moment you are moved to this level of completion within you, then you can move to **WE**, the One.

Then, in stillness you move on, forward through the timeless corridor of Self.

This meeting point is now.

Here and now you find yourselves in the magic moment of this unfolding purpose.

WE, you are,

WE, you exist within the timeless, limitless state of Being.

WE, you have come to find your way back to another form of Self; to remember the flow of purpose that is Self.

I receive me fully and as I do, this and everything else around me lines up perfectly within 'the moment', within the One.

Here is my full purpose of being that fluid energy, fluid forms of light consciousness.

Here you are, this is you that has been holding you within all time, within 'the moment' forever.

EE AHHH,   NAE EE TAH,   SEENNN AHHH

Chalice Activation

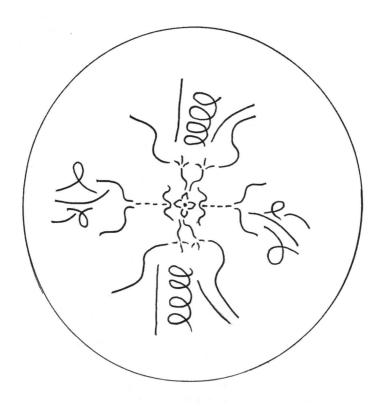

Sound: DAHST EE....

CHAPTER 6
BRIDGING THE GAP

Through the initiations we have completed in the previous chapters we have realigned ourselves into another level of our spiritual evolution. Through these processes we have come to a deeper understanding of our place within the Universal Community, and by doing so have entered a new realm of our spiritual home and connection to Self. Through these experiences of "taking our place," there has been a further revelation of our own purpose and the unique part that we each are to play now on the earth plane and within the Universes. This clarity brings a spiritual maturity, an in-depth understanding of the significance of our purpose and mission. Our individual journey within this incarnation has prepared us to fully engage and embark on this destined path.

We do not have specific step-by-step details of how we are to reach our destination, simply because the details of the journey are irrelevant from the Higher Realm perspective. Rather than focusing on "the destination," we need to be involved with our current journey. What is essential to any process is to take one step at a time, trusting each moment, knowing a sacred unfolding is taking place within us. Understanding that the moment within our journey reveals everything when we allow ourselves to be in an open state of "receivership." We always know that our ego mind, which is fully connected to illusion on this planet, will try to break down the moment due to a lack of appreciation for any aspect of this phase of our journey that is outside the illusion.

There is a call going out for us to surrender! This surrendering is to a higher part of Self and requires letting go of what we think we know, and even what we consider as Truth. As we are willing to open into allowing everything to fall away, we can then access a doorway filled with unlimited possibilities. Our need to know, our need to understand, sources directly from the ego mind. This is the mind holding strong elements of attachment, illusion, and limitation. As we move into acceptance of not having the answers, we are able to enter the unlimited realms of possibilities and potential of Self.

As we open into an unlimited space that "letting go" reveals, we can become totally engaged and guided by our own Higher Self. Through this act of choosing to let go of knowing, we move out of separation and into liberation, fully embracing and aligning to the moment that opens. We are able to access the multidimensional potential and allow a clear connection to guidance from our Higher Self that will steer us impeccably on our paths.

We have been going through a strong birthing process, realigning to aspects of our multifaceted dimensionality of Higher Realm elements. We have been drawn back through the pure conscious vibrations, like a current in a river taking us, returning us Home to reconnect to our original makeup. We have gone through powerful recalibrations through our new Blueprint, which has activated a natural anchoring process for us to align to Home. These pure frequencies from the Blueprint are continuously transforming the cells, so we begin to anchor the light through our physical bodies. This action has supported the birthing process of bringing the heavenly frequencies into existence on the earth plane through our transformation.

This anchoring has always been an essential aspect of our mission, bringing heaven on earth in this lifetime. This is part of our destiny. The full journey of our transformation involves many steps within the different levels of self-discovery. One step is not more important than another; each step is vital to our evolutionary process. Now we are ready for another movement that will bring us to a place where we can flow unencumbered by any third-dimensional blocks. This step will be a natural accelerator of our enlightenment process.

Our humanness is elemental to creating the completion of Self. We have yet to fully evolve through to the greatest aspect of our humanness: compassion and love. These key ingredients naturally begin to evolve through a building awareness of the very existence of our Higher Self. By opening into this frequency of Truth, which is a foundation of the sacred within us, we are able to examine, then embrace this new higher experience of Self that exists beyond illusion. The transformational journey of our human nature birthing solidarity with our Higher Self is the goal.

We have come to this earth plane to have the full human experience. Now we move forward and begin an awakening process through this alignment with our Higher Self. This phase entails a transformational relationship with our humanness and at the same time a conscious connection to our sacred Self. We are to attain our fully enlightened state while still in our physical form.

We have been on a journey of self-exploration of our higher nature for our awakening, moving between the illusions of the ego mind and the energy of the spiritual world. Swinging from a spiritual connection to Self and then being plummeted back by our human ego mind into the illusion. This has been our process—like an out-of-control teeter-totter, going back and forth between our spiritual experience and the human experience, unable to depend on any constant stability within our sacred connections.

Gradually we have been forging ahead, gaining deeper understandings, learning, and unfolding through our alignments to Self. We have been rebuilding a relationship to our own inner sacredness, toward a new flow with our intuitive aspect of Self. This revolutionary process has been a huge learning curve, as we have had to adjust to the existence of the new dimensional settings that continue to be revealed within us and within our lives. We are evolving as if drawn by an invisible current into these series of remembering processes that have brought us into deeper levels of maturity and awareness of Self. As we realign into the frequency of Truth our sacred places are unveiled, bringing us into a more stable connection to our true spiritual Home.

Within the full transformational journey of our spiritual birthing there is the necessity for us to begin to explore a deeper root core connection to our humanness. Our human element holds essential aspects of the whole within our completion energy. It carries the vast pure potential of the self-realized human expression of love. This is a foundation of Truth. Love is fundamental in building and fortifying a necessary base within us, enabling the full anchoring of this frequency of love. Our Higher Self can fulfill the role of providing this base, which can be initiated as we consciously activate the process of merging, creating a sacred union between our human aspect and our spiritual Self.

Many of us have done extensive inner work to support the transition of our awakening. We are being called right now to investigate where we are still holding any remnants of separation within us. We need to delve on a deeper level through an introspection process to be able to move into a more authentic and healthy relationship with our human aspect. Each individual process of introspection is liberating and empowering. Resolving separation elements within us brings an end to the internal wars. The internal conflicts continue where emotional distress still exists or in which we are still holding onto a victim role.

Dealing with these remnants of unresolved feelings within us brings a release of any remaining barriers, ending the separation elements created by our self-judgment. This allows us to have a more profound access to our full heart space. We can then re-inhabit areas of our heart that have previously been closed, reopening the door so we can return once more to the Home space of the Higher Self.

The Pleiadians say that enlightenment can only come through our self-acceptance. This means embracing all the unique pieces of our journey and honoring all the decisions and experiences from our life. Every aspect of our self needs to be received by us, including the shadow side and the glorious side. One is not more than the other. Everything is just an experience.

The misconception, the illusion has been that in order to become enlightened we needed to be perfect. We have been chasing after this perfection in ourselves. The Pleiadians say, "As a human being we are perfectly imperfect." There is no chance of us achieving perfection. Imperfection is a human condition! We have been created this way in order to have our full learning experience. They often remind us that in order to move into our enlightenment we simply need to move into a state of acceptance of ourselves, just as we are in this moment. Through acceptance we automatically move into a state of self-love. Self-acceptance is self-love.

When we are in separation from our selves we are automatically isolated from every other human being. Through self-judgment we can't allow ourselves to receive the love. We can't allow ourselves to receive the abundance of success. We sabotage ourselves from receiving our heart's desire. We are alone and yet there is a yearning within us to be accepted and included. Our life is the mirror, reflecting how we are treating ourselves inside through the constant self-judgments. As we move into self-acceptance the internal separation can end. Separation brings a deep suffering and isolation within, keeping us from experiencing that part which is sacred.

A harshness exists within the ego mind, which moves quickly into a state of judging. We hold judgments of our past within us, and we create an unending cycle of self-condemnation. There is a subtlety in many of the actions of the ego mind, a sabotaging that can hardly be perceived. Without realizing it, we become the voice of our parents long after they have left us. We become the perpetrator of the negative traits that people have assigned to us, those who gave us the subtle or not so subtle messages about ourselves.

The ego mind can only source from that which has taken place in the past. With the past as its only reference point, the ego perpetuates fear and negativity. The ego continues an onslaught of criticism that we have grown up with, repeating negative messages that we received as a child. Constantly asking questions and demanding answers, the ego has a huge appetite and is addicted to "the need to understand." The Truth is the ego mind is not capable of understanding anything beyond the third-dimensional illusion.

The ego mind has a need to be right in order to stay in control of all situations. Trying "to be right" creates a barrier within our own heart, disconnecting us from all that is intuitive within. This need prevents spontaneity and any authentic interaction in many areas of life. While we are focused on an agenda of being right, we miss all opportunities of being in the moment.

In order to successfully move into our enlightenment experience, we need to end all internal separation. This breakdown has been created by us and can be transformed by us. The ego mind has a misinterpretation of what our journey is about, and will never understand what we have come to experience and achieve in this lifetime.

We have not come here to maintain the limited belief systems of our families or of society, or those we have inherited from previous generations. This was where we began in our journey. We have come to embark on a self-liberating journey of reconnecting and rediscovering that which is authentic within. We set this goal in place before coming into this incarnation.

We need to change any old dynamics that are still playing out through the interactions with our human part. By opening up a new level of authenticity with our selves, for our selves, we bring nourishment in the form of a loving, nurturing, and healing balm.

We must find the courage to move forward and be willing to reopen the doors we have closed. Nobody has forced us to close doors within our heart. We have made decisions, made choices at certain junctures within the different experiences we have encountered in life. We have shut down our hearts in moments of deep despair and pain. These closures have been to save ourselves from the pain, rejection, and betrayals. Now it is time to move fully beyond these self-inflicted constraints.

The transformation of our relationship with our own human ego brings to us a new potential. As we break down the existing barriers within us, the illusions can shift. These barriers, which have held the illusion steadily in place, have held us back from a full and stable experience with our Higher Self.

This is the time to move into a state of honest resolution with the human part of our self. The first step toward acceptance of our selves on a human level is to begin to explore and understand the Truth of the purpose of our human journey here on the planet. To ask ourselves the right questions.

There has been some discussion previously of the dynamic of our unique journey that we have lived. The series of individual paths we have chosen to take, the decisions we have made, the processes we have experienced. All of our experiences were designed to enable us to fulfill our learning process. There has been no wrong turn in the road, just a series of life challenges that we needed, that we created for ourselves. Our life has been a perfectly divine orchestration by our Higher Self to ensure we each achieve our unique human experience. This is a Truth.

We are not responsible for anyone else's experience, only our own. We play out our full experience, and so does everyone else. All of our collective experiences were perfectly designed for us. You see why there can be no regrets with the decisions we have made, there can be no guilt for any of our actions, and there can be no shame from our choices.

We have all done the very best we could in each moment of time, playing out our roles fully and having our experiences. That is what we have come here to do up to this point. If we perceive any self-condemnation, any regret, or just a small emotional discomfort around an issue, this unease is an indicator that there are still unresolved emotions within us that is creating a separating element. We are committing to an ongoing exploration of the judgments about ourselves as they arise, and to make changes. I get excited when I come across some of these inner twinges because I know that I am about to liberate myself on another level.

Mother Mary appeared to me one day to show me how I was creating a deflecting process when I opened up to receive. She demonstrated this to me by transmitting light to me, and I could witness an internal holding on. This was my deflecting shield in place, interfering in my ability to being able to fully receive. She stayed with me, guiding me into letting go as she continued to bathe me in the light. I witnessed myself as I let go of the striving. I could feel a deep shift of an old belief system of "not deserving" begin to fall away. This was a profound, emotionally moving process that enabled the light to enter my being. I witnessed the barriers in my heart that I had constructed long ago melt away, allowing a pure form of light to re-enter. With the release of this block my relationship with my human self was able to transform. I was able to manifest in my life my heart's desire and move forward with a new lightness of Being. Letting go is a basic tool that can bring us back into self-empowerment and full self-liberation.

Look inside and know your self. There is power and freedom in being familiar with your vulnerabilities and idiosyncrasies. We are not looking for perfection, only self-acceptance. If there are feelings of betrayal, we are playing a victim role. This is a strongly played-out role for many, being part of the illusion on the planet. While we remain a victim we cannot heal. We need to take responsibility for the lead role we have played on our stage.

In order to end our internal separation, we need only focus on the Truth held within the different segments of our lives that still get our attention. This can be through emotional reactions, or just an individual issue coming to mind. This response is telling us that something is unresolved within us. We can then explore the issues, to absolve ourselves and anyone else of any wrong doing, because of the Truth.

Opening into this Truth of our journey, we get to know that we are really okay. We have done nothing wrong, and more importantly there is nothing wrong with us. Deep inside ourselves we have had the belief that we are really not okay and this has been perpetuated by criticism of others and then through our own self-judgment.

Remember that we chose to take on these messages about ourselves, and now an essential part of our process is to take ownership of these messages we have given to ourselves.

As we begin to open into an authentic relationship with our human part we will encounter a profound relief within us. Once we meet our deepest fears about ourselves, peace can reside within and the internal war can cease. The suffering, the internal separation, can end.

The good news is we have free will to choose to do things differently. We are allowed to change our minds and choose again for our selves. We can rewrite how we receive ourselves, how we play out our lives from this point on. As we begin to liberate ourselves from the barriers within, we can evolve and open into this new potential of our humanity.

This inner process will allow an authentic state of relationship with Self, allowing us to move back to a state of balance through this revival of an honest and intimate connection with our human part. As we choose to meet ourselves in this way, our human element can flourish.

Now is the time to bring the compassion and understanding of our journey out into the full light of Truth, to begin to acknowledge our own courage within the experiences from this viewpoint. As we let go of the role of judge, we can become the compassionate witness of ourselves. We can honor the complete role that we have played out in this lifetime. Honor our sacred journey and "perfectly imperfect" design. Hold our human element in all the different phases, visiting the multifaceted experiences within our glorious journeys. And most importantly, feel the depth of compassion for ourselves and all that we have experienced.

Our human experience is not over. Actually, it is just beginning. There is a rite of passage being revealed to move us toward the full potential of our humanity. For this next phase we are being called to begin a sacred forging between our human aspect and Higher Self. Through the forming of an energetic bridge we will launch the energy of this rite of passage.

Our human aspect will be the anchor for the earth and our Higher Self will establish the heavenly contact.

This Bridging will create a sacred communion that will expand and enhance our human potential. This enlightenment process is about re-union. Together the heaven and earth components of our self become One as this collective synergy is forged through the Bridge. Through the Bridge our Higher Self and human aspect make up this union point of light that fully engages a sacred synergy with the Collective God Consciousness. This is our completion energy, forever unfolding this sacred wholeness within us.

As we begin to work within some of the aspects that create the separating element within us, this Bridging process will naturally begin to open. The process of Bridging must be a conscious choosing initiated by each one of us, done in alliance with our Higher Self. We need to consciously open up a pathway to build this Bridge from the heavenly aspect of your Higher Self, to the earthly aspect of our human part. Initially the Bridge brings to our human element a holding of pure vibrational love from the heavens of the Higher Self. This love bathes the sphere of the human consciousness, which enables an acceleration of the awakening process. This supportive energy helps us move and navigate through the last remnants of our self-imposed separation because through the light we can perceive Truth. And with the love we can forge into the depth of our human vulnerability.

As the Bridge begins to unfold, the heavenly aspect of your Higher Self continues to enliven and nurture the human aspect, bringing a depth of peace and understanding with the essential essence of love that the human part requires to mature and flourish. This begins to anchor the Bridge through the human aspect and into the earthly realm. There is a deep acceptance and love that begins to evolve with the Higher Self and human aspect, bringing more essential nutrients of love to the human aspect. The Bridge process anchors the heaven-earth connection through this journey. This unfolding of the Bridge is glorious, like the bud of a flower opening to the Sun, with the human aspect fully blossoming.

When I began to consciously choose to build this Bridge my whole human experience transformed. I began by being given the understanding that as I engaged with my Higher Self energy I needed to consciously open my human part to the experience of that energy as it was happening. I would feel the deepening connection take place from my Higher Self, and then would consciously bring my human part into the peace, the love, and the feeling of freedom. Through each individual experience with these encounters my human part was deeply changed; it was amazing and profound to feel a quietness and peace that had not been previously present. My bridge grew with each conscious encounter.

I began to witness the miracle of this love working within my human element, where a daily transformation began to occur. Profound healing took place with many old wounds and suffering from my past human experiences falling away. This love brought to me a deep, peaceful stability within my human part. I was able to move into living life feeling free from a heaviness that I felt was a part of me. I experienced a lifting of the fear and came into knowing that I was really okay. I also became aware of a new sense of strengthening in my physical body. It was as if my physical cells were being fed by the frequency of light of love that was bathing me through the Bridge.

At a certain moment my human part began to acknowledge the Bridge, and there was an anchoring of the Bridge through my earthly aspect as I began to consciously participate on a continual basis with my Higher Self.

A trust grew between that human part and my Higher Self. As the Bridge became more evolved between my humanness and Higher Self, I was able to experience more of the love that was there within me—that human part. Because of the love I was receiving directly from Self, my human aspect began to comprehend life as it was in Truth. This led to an honoring of my self-acceptance of my own profound journey in all of its shades as a human being. I was able to hold all aspects within me and appreciate my full journey. This entire process brought a huge internal relief, knowing that I had moved toward Home intact, with no separation, just Being.

Change is here and the changing dynamic needs to be inside of us because in Truth everything is internal. There is nothing that we cannot achieve because we hold the sacred that we are within. There is no outer tool that we require to achieve all that we have come here to experience and complete. We rely on no other human being, and there is nothing that is not within our ability to accomplish.

Our role now is to support ourselves moving into self-empowerment. For us to achieve this we need to come back into that place of balance with our human aspect through the Bridge. As we transform in this relationship with our human aspect, self-love opens a great potential within us to carry a depth of compassion and empathy for other human beings.

We as a human being have this incredible potential to hold a new frequency of ourselves as we begin to evolve through our Bridge into a deep inner communion to our Higher Self. We can begin to receive the frequency of unconditional love through this Bridge. It is our time to live differently: free from the fear, the separation, and the limitations of feeling small and insignificant. We can begin to witness that which we are in our entirety. We can embrace all the multidimensional levels of our selves as we end this internal war and open up the Bridge. We can let go of the barriers within us, opening up to our unlimited potential to Be. This is our time to come back into an authentic alignment to our sacredness as a human being.

Through our human transformation we now have the sacred inner tools for us to establish a New Dawning Community on our planet Earth. As we move into our full self-realization as human beings we can bring the true compassion and unconditional love to form a sacred communion within Communities. Within this communion the ego mind will no longer reign and we will build connections with each other through our compassionate hearts. Each individual will be supported, honored for what they bring through their own individual frequency of being, understanding that each one of us holds a uniqueness that is necessary for the flourishing of the Community energy. Competition of the ego will cease to exist and our Bridges will allow for each one of us to move into the sacred knowingness of this time. Together we will form this sacred synergy, a collective union of trust based on Truth from within.

Note: You can find an audio file link at *www.christinedayonline.com/pleiadianpromise* This audio file will support your ongoing process of connection and building your heaven and earth connections through your Bridge.

CHAPTER 7
RETRIEVING THE KEYS

The transformational energy of the New Dawning is flowing across our earth plane like a gale force wind, bringing the energy of a brilliant frequency of light consciousness. This pure frequency flows within all crevices and merges into the Earth. It is absorbed through every minute and intricate form of nature that exists within our planet and simultaneously infiltrates the spaces within our physical cells. This light energy disperses and interacts through the multidimensional realities that exist on this earth plane. Opening up and exposing the different states of reality, that in truth have always co-existed with us as humans, and that we, on higher levels, are a natural part. We are ready to embark on a new expansive grand adventure with Self.

We have been through a series of extreme initiations in order to be ready to begin to navigate ourselves into a higher, more expansive realm. We move ourselves forward to enter into a new vista of multidimensionality. Remember: We are multidimensional beings, and yes, we have up to this point been limited by our human experience. The timing is right for us to move into this new rhythm of vibration that naturally holds and weaves through our multidimensional states of being. We begin a more expansive journey of self-retrieval through initiations into a series of various frequency signatures. These signatures carry a vastly different dimensional aspect of Self than we have encountered within our current history of the planet.

We stand poised on the edge of a cliff and we are being asked to let go, to leap into the abyss. As I entered this phase of profound change, the Pleiadians asked me, "How will you ever use your wings if you don't jump off the cliff? How will you ever know you can fly?"

This is our time to shift into a very different element of Self—to take yet another "turn in the road" and reposition ourselves to another level of our sacredness.

Our natural makeup is held within a sacred design, which is made up of many unlimited facets that carry the pure frequency states of our Being. Within these facets lies our pure consciousness form that holds enormous potential. Now is the time for us to enter our full sacred design of enlightenment. Up to this point we have not fully interacted and anchored with some of our more expanded states of consciousness that make up the fullness of our spiritual character. We are unfamiliar with the higher aspect of our heritage states, which make up a large part of our consciousness. As we begin this next phase of moving into this birthing process we will reclaim and inhabit these heritage states that exist, realigning back to a dynamic aspect of our completed consciousness.

We, as a human race, have not been aware of the existence of these expanded states of consciousness, nor have we been able to fully appreciate who we are in our totality within the wholeness of Self. This is the time we move forward and take back the full multidimensional ownership of the sacred that we are.

A Message From the Galactic Community

Beloved ones,

We, the Pleiadians, are here in the moment to hand you access to the Keys that exist within what is called the Krae Records. These Keys hold the full completion energies of awakening for you. They will give you access to an unveiling of the full multidimensional essence of Self that has existed through all time. Up until this moment we have not been able to even speak of these expanded multidimensional states that exist within you. The time has come for us to begin to reveal the existence of these sacred aspects and begin to transmit the energy of these vibrational states to you. We begin sending this transmission out to you now, through the written word. As you read this sacred text there is an automatic frequency transmission of Truth birthing through you right now! Your heart cells receive this transmission and open instantly, recognizing and receiving this Truth. You may become aware of a quickening taking place through your heart cells as you open to this Truth.

These profound energies have been held in place waiting for this time of revelation. For this is the exact moment in your evolution as a human race to embark on this transformational journey of discovery. This is the moment to begin to receive this potent and expanded multidimensional potential that has always existed as an essential part of you, as a natural part of your birthright. This will be the most important step of your destiny up to this point, retrieving the Keys through the space of the Krae Records.

This expanded form of Self does not exist within your physical form yet; however, there is a natural interaction between your heart and this expanded multidimensional energy form of Self. The expanded form of your essence is currently being held within our Keys within the Records until the moment you choose to retrieve your Keys. Your own multidimensional heart space carries a powerful link directly to the Keys. Your heart plays an essential role as it holds an energetic space for your fully awakened essence to come Home. There is a knowing awareness of this expanded dimensional energetic form of Self within your heart.

Our role is to bring to you that which is sacred Knowledge that has been part of a weaving that is contained within the Krae Records. We have been waiting for your readiness to proceed forward into your unfolding initiation. You are now in a direct alignment to begin to retrieve your Keys through the space of the Krae Records.

These understandings will support you in being able to let go, and move with conscious knowingness of the rightness of these next steps for you. We are here to guide you in this completion journey. By bringing these Truths forward we can assist you in this profound initiation process. Together we enter this next transitional phase.

This happening brings us great joy. We witness you as you are enabled to open into a deeper understanding of your power and your true place within the Collective Consciousness. We honor you as you move forward into this unfolding of Self.

Blessings,

The Pleiadians

We will be assisted with locating the Krae Records and through the records be able to access our individual Keys. This activation of the Keys opens the floodgates of a full living vibration of our multidimensional essence. Simultaneously there will be a deep and profound sense of "knowing" released through us. This clarity will explode through our senses. It is imperative that in that moment we let go, allowing a huge tidal wave to take us and reposition us to our original settings. The Christ energy will be present in that energetic moment. As we move through this rapid resurrection process we will be aligning to our light consciousness on a vastly different consciousness level. This expanded frequency of Self aligns us into an aspect of our multidimensionality, bringing us back to the awareness that we have always been, through all time.

As we move into this higher expression of Self we will become a part of the expanded collective energy that has always existed. This Collective Consciousness is woven throughout many Universes that exist within a Central Sun. The Collective Consciousness is waiting to receive us in our fullness, and, more importantly, this collective energy has been waiting to be received by us.

Moving through this Central Sun we encounter the existence of the God Seat of Power. This God Seat is the central consciousness that exists through all life forms within the entire collection of Universes. As we go through our rapid evolution with the activation of our Keys we will begin to energetically emerge like a butterfly leaving our cocoon. We will be drawn into the initiation of the Central Sun and then will fully align to this God Seat of Power energy. This alignment will be a fully conscious experience. We will simply remember the full expression of love that emanates from the God Seat. Through this conscious reconnection we will begin to enter a transmutation process, transforming through our own newly aligned sacred consciousness state, within the divine central core of Self. This will be a sacred emergence that will allow us to feel our own holy presence in alignment to all life force in the Universe. Within this expanded union space we will be enlivened and thrive.

Working with our Keys will need to be initiated through a pure source layered component that is carried within the different segments of the Keys. Opening entry points to build and birth our multidimensional frequency. This will be played out one frequency setting at a time, which will enable the pure force of our light to gradually emanate through our physical and energetic systems. There are a series of initiations with the Keys that we will need to release within us. We will become the initiator of our own birthing process. Unfolding into our sacred multidimensionality Self within the unlimited moment so that we can carry a pure flame of our light within, which is referred to as the "inner torch."

Each aspect of the Keys carries a unique, multidimensional frequency of our highest nature. The Keys carry a series of pure light particles that hold the finest and most sacred forms of Truth. We will be working with these series of light particles, one particle at a time. Each light particle held within the Keys will enhance and unfold within the physical form of every cell that exists within our physical body. There will be an opening of a sacred multidimensional consciousness within the cells as each light particle is expressed through us. This expression of energy will enable us to interact through the higher multidimensional states that we exist within naturally. Through this reconnection to our full existence, we will express our individual place within the entire collective energies of all the Universes.

This is our time to align to the frequency of understanding that is being transmitted through the fullness of the New Dawning light. This has always existed, and now we will be able to perceive all that is in existence within the Higher Realms. There is a meeting point that awaits us to support our higher mission, so as we retrieve our Keys we remember fully that which we have pre-agreed to fulfill for humanity within our missions.

There are some essential points we need to be aware of in receiving ourselves within this transformational process. As we begin to move into the sacred dynamic of the Keys, we must open up to fully participate and consciously engage within each facet of our unfolding. This understanding will enable us to more fully embrace the next step of our work within the energies held through the individual layers within the Keys.

Our authentic power is found within our Keys. We need to be prepared to relinquish all that we think we are, and all that we think we know, in order to move our selves fully into this new realm of existence. We need to be prepared to allow everything from this earth plane to simply drop away from us during this initial step and we must stand free from all earthly connections as we move through the entry point to our Keys.

These energetic Keys hold our individual connection to our Sacred. They carry the unique link that opens directly through to the depth of our own light consciousness. The Keys contain the sacred aspect of our central divine Core. In Truth, they have never been separate from us. We have been disconnected, until this time in our destiny.

Our original heritage energy that is contained within these Keys has been hidden, existing in a multidimensional form that is held beyond the Timeline of Earth. The energy of Earth has not been able to anchor the pure force of energy that exists within our Keys up until this time. Within this same Timeless space beyond Earth, our Keys are anchored, carrying our unique divine imprint for our full self-realization. The initiations are completed through the sum total of a series of individual pure light particles.

Each light particle holds an initiation process to open up an aspect of our full heritage of awakening. These individual light particles work by expanding through the central divine Core that will eventually anchor within our Home Space. We are able to access and align to these initiations because of the imprint of consciousness that makes up an aspect of our Blueprint. Our new Blueprint that is currently active holds the entire frequency code that is necessary for our complete initiation with each light particle.

Our Keys have always resonated to the frequency of our multidimensional central divine Core. This Core is an aspect of us that has resided outside of our physical body until now and we have simply been unaware of this particular aspect of our existence.

As we open through our Keys and begin our initiation through the individual light particles, there will be a repositioning of our Core. Our Core will re-establish itself within our Home Space of our heart center. Our Core holds our totality, interacting directly with the God Seat energy that is woven through all life forms within the Collective Universes. Within this completed state we will align fully through the one Central Sun that holds all life force alongside the God Seat energy. Know that through the Keys we will naturally realign back into an authentic interaction to the Central Sun.

We have a main energetic Framework within us that is multidimensional in form. This Framework is linked to our current active Blueprint. Our new Blueprint holds the matching design for our awakening through our Keys. The Blueprint sustains the frequency that allows us to reconnect to the Keys. This Framework supports us in launching into the different multidimensional settings that are held in the individual initiations within the Keys.

Our Framework encompasses our energetic field and holds us within a pure form, like an energetic womb. It plays the role of a strong anchor to enable us to stabilize as we align through the energy of the dimensional space where the Krae Records exist. This Framework maintains our energetic balance and allows us to experience and integrate into our full initiation as we access and are received through the light particles held within our Keys. This energetic force contained within the Keys operates very differently than any other energetic form that we have encountered so far in our unfolding initiations. The Keys can only operate because of the existence of our energetic Framework that forms an energetic-like womb around us.

We will be drawing from our current Blueprint form as we enter the Krae Records. Our Blueprint carries the completion of our destiny point, mirroring all that exists through this new frequency lifeline.

As we activate a light particle layer within our Keys there will be a potent release of a frequency form that will contain a precise energetic purpose. There is a purity held within this energetic force that contains a vibrating brilliance. There is first an opening, and then like an explosion, there is a quickening action that anchors an inner torch, like a pure form of a flame. This is an instantaneous happening, a birthing that is taking place within our consciousness, carrying monumental significance. This is the action of an awakening of these pure light particles.

This specific initiation process is simply pure light. We absorb the energy held and released through the pure light particle within our Keys. The phrase "blinded by the light" is a very accurate description of this profound alignment and integration process of the awakening that takes place within us. The moment we enter this birth, there is a simultaneous repositioning of the central divine Core into our Home Space, and the inner flame opens up through the Core.

The purpose of the flame has a designed mission, which is multidimensional and carries a layered level of light consciousness within. This flame flows into our own central divine Core, and through the Core it will be released to interact through the individual cells of our body. Our cells will absorb the pureness of the love that this flame ignites through us. This quality form of love will explode light through our consciousness, propelling us through a dimensional doorway to meet our heritage Self.

Our Framework will interact through the cells of our body and monitor the expanded level of light that will be flowing within us. This interaction by our Framework will support our complete integration process of each individual initiation. The unfolding of this process allows us to fully encompass our newly birthed purity. This gives us an avenue to experience our multidimensional light consciousness state that is being released from our initiation with each pure light particle held within the Keys. The cells will then be able to fully absorb our new frequency Self, and create a direct experience of awakening.

We have been in a limited multidimensional setting through this present phase of our awakening. Yes, we have been in an unfolding process with Self, this is true. However, we have been unaware of the many limitations that have been imposed upon us. These have been preventing us from moving into a deeper, more authentic connection to Self and outwardly to the rest of the Universal Community.

This limitation has been a necessary factor in order for us to consolidate our human interactions with our sacred natures. We have been pulled back to ensure that the energy within our own consciousness is prepared to fully engage with these profound heritage spaces of experience. There is also a destiny timing involved with this next step process, as planet Earth was not destined to carry these higher frequencies of evolution until now.

The Krae Records contain our Keys, and hold our energetic records. These records reside within a Timeless multidimensional space that is anchored, layered, and held as a frequency library. Many other records are also being stored within this dimensionally layered space. All of the Akashic Records exist there. There are an unlimited number of energetic libraries that contain all the pure consciousness knowledge held in the form of these energetic frequencies.

This Knowledge is for the utilization of the entire Universes. They are made up into a series of combined dimensional settings that have been energetically engineered to be arranged through individual dimensional positions for our accessing. This Knowledge is freely given to all those who are ready to receive the different levels of teaching.

As we evolve, we are given access to activate these frequencies of Knowledge within us. These libraries will create a powerful impact in our lives as a Community. As we are individually ready to utilize the force of light that this Knowledge contains we will play our essential role. Holding this Knowledge within us will open a new horizon for our future Communities. This sacred Knowledge will play a major role in the coming times. Each one of us will be given individual access to support humanity at the right moment.

The Community of Light within all the collective Universes will be strongly impacted by our journey of retrieving our Keys. We will actively contribute within the existence of this New Dawning time, through our full connection to the collective God Seat of Power.

Earth will go through a series of transformations. These changes are predestined and involve a complete metamorphic reset within the vibration of the planet. Through our fully awakened frequency that we will carry within us, there will be a new design of an energetic network birthed around and throughout the planet. We will be instrumental in anchoring this network because of the newly designed energy that we will carry within us.

This energetic network will support the forming of the new Communities that will be developed throughout our earth plane. There will be a sacred webbing that is part of this network that will begin to be woven within Communities. This weaving will open and expose the dense areas within the planet, releasing any density that has been strongly holding the illusion in place. This will support the letting go of the old ways, enabling humankind to step into the higher and lighter realms that exist beyond the illusion.

Through this dynamic opening of our individual communion to the God Seat, a Sacred Trust will extend between each one of us who has initiated through our Keys. We will be carrying the divine essence of God within us, and that essence will be interwoven through all of the collective life force energies on our planet, impacting all of humanity's potential to Be.

There will be many of us in this highly transformed state and together we will hold the energy to form a new paradigm on the Earth. Our united communion alignment to the God Seat will create a sacred weaving through the planet, breaking down the barriers of illusion and bringing a joyful reunion between us.

As this transformation evolves the energies of the Central Sun will finally begin to touch the Earth with its energetic rays, aligning through the Earth, weaving a new life force frequency within the natural forces. This will herald in a new beginning for our Earth and humankind.

Note: You can find an audio file link at *www.christinedayonline.com/pleiadianpromise*

1.   Retrieving the Keys—Sound: AE NATAH (page 128)

Let's look at how we are going to begin this amazing process of retrieving our Keys. You will access your Keys through a channeled process. This is a simple process of listening to the audio file, and working within the patterning that has been entrusted to you. You will always have your Retrieving the Keys patterning circle in front of you when you work with the audio file.

I will be guiding you step by step. You will work with the audio file many times. The patterning will move you into the individual "pure light particles" that will lead you into your awakened states. You will work with only one pure light particle within your Keys in any one journey.

The audio file is designed as a multidimensional document, which means that each time you take the journey it will be different. Each time you listen to the audio file you will access higher frequencies of your Keys. Each time you listen to the audio file you will be carrying a higher frequency of Self. The initiation energies are unlimited and so are you. Enjoy the journey!

Retrieving the Keys

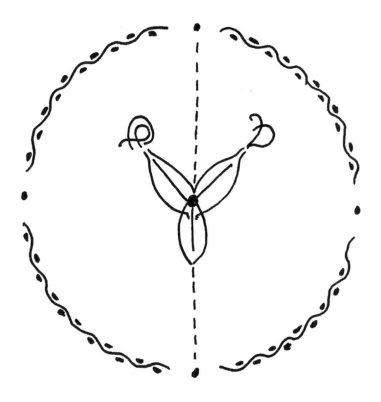

Sound: AE NATAH

CHAPTER 8
CLAIMING YOUR SACRED HERITAGE

There is a pervasive and omnipotent consciousness that originates far beyond our Earth and our resident Universe. This pure consciousness filters through to each one of us within our resident Universe. This source of light embodies the collective energy of a series of alternative Universes that exist and make up what is called the God Seat of Power. This all-encompassing source of light consciousness sits at the very center of the creation element, within its own multidimensional structure and embodies the purest frequencies of Knowledge.

These alternative Universes collectively hold the platform for us to move into the self-realization of our sacred heritage. This is simply because we exist within this collective energy through our own higher multidimensional state. These Universes play a major role in our enlightenment process. They hold the sacred on our behalf and they anchor the full Knowledge to enable an active platform to exist. Our heritage is intertwined within this central platform within these Universes. And the very nature of the collective frequency of our individual sacred heritage is calling us Home.

Now is the time for us to rediscover our true expanded natures, our true heritage so that we begin to perceive where we exist on a multi-dimensional level within this Collective Consciousness within these Universes. There is an essential need for us to come into an understanding of the geography of our planet Earth in relationship to the rest of these Universes. It is imperative for us to own our place within this collective Family of Light and for us to begin to embrace our spiritual roots so that we can actively return to that which we have always belonged.

Through this perspective and understanding of the expansive nature of ourselves we will be propelled forward to leap into the abyss, consciously choosing to take flight as we reopen into the powerful reconnections that are a natural part of our spiritual heritage within these Universes. We emerge, like a butterfly from the cocoon, finally finding our wings, taking flight and returning Home into the light of Truth of Self that has been waiting to receive us.

It is essential for us to change our perspective of ourselves, and of our planet Earth within this amazing and all-encompassing network that does exist within the Collective Universes. Through this new viewpoint of our selves we will move purposefully toward our completed heritage state. This is our time for our complete renewal!

We cannot ignore these higher aspects of our heritage and as we evolve within our connections we will initiate further into our original imprint. We need to extend our awareness outward because our consciousness exists and thrives well beyond this earth plane and our Universe. Home extends well beyond Earth, outward into our resident Universe, and then further, flowing further into extended Universes.

As we grasp and open into this whole concept of our true geographical environment and the true scope of our lineage connections there is an innate expression of awakening that activates within us. Through our Home Space into our Core there are a series of initiations that will be activated, giving us direct access to a doorway through the central platform that has been held. This will bring us into an alignment to begin to source from the hierarchy that exists within the Universes.

There is a heralding in of this profound time of unveiling, as we are able to open into a true orientation of the position we hold within the Collective. Through this awareness there will be a new pathway in which we can embark. There will be the unveiling of a next step of our journey as these new understandings are imparted toward us, through us from the Platform. From these revelations we will be given access to move forward through this clarity, then experiencing this new element of landscape that we actually exist within. Through Truth being received we will be empowered to engage within this sacred weaving that our spiritual heritage entitles us.

It has been difficult for us to reemerge into this reality of Truth. We have been so Earth bound for lifetimes, being immersed with the full illusion and limitation of ourselves on this planet. We each hold within us an unlimited form of consciousness that extends and interacts throughout all of the Universes naturally. We are each interwoven within the sacred network of light consciousness that moves through infinity.

This new orientation of our surroundings will "unearth" us, set us free from the bonds of our earth plane, which has kept us anchored in our limitation of who we are, where we have claim to have existed up to now, and where we imagine we have originated from.

As we open to Truth, we are moving ourselves into a different dimensional perception of our true existence. Know that our conscious acceptance begins a conscious journey. We start another path of engaging energetically within the Collective Community within these Universes. Through this act of consciously opening we begin a transformational journey of liberation and authenticity from another dimensional perspective.

Through our unfolding of this expanded perception of Self we will begin to glimpse another aspect of our existence beyond Earth, to our own resident Universe, and through to our full role within the Collective Universes. This allows us to finally emerge from the cocoon of illusion, from the restriction that has been the basis of our creation here on the earth plane. We begin a completion aspect of our resurrection through accessing a much bigger picture of what is Truth, setting in motion a profound process of alignment to our spiritual heritage.

Our evolution requires that we begin to move our awareness outward to meet the multidimensional sacred part of Self that extends far beyond

Earth, well beyond this neighborhood that is our resident Universe. This is an essential part of our destiny plan. The full energy of this plan is held within our Blueprint that we now carry. We are to build our communion connections to our resident Universal Community, and at the same time, have our extended consciousness touching our sacred heritage path within the expanded Universes. There is only the Oneness. This interconnection is a natural extension of the sacred that we are.

A larger part of our focus in this lifetime has been Earth bound, which has been necessary for us to fulfill the journey of our human experience. However, an enormous space of unlimited potential is opening up to us now through our engagement with the other world realities beyond our planet Earth. We each carry an individual aspect of the God Consciousness, which is held within the Oneness element. This is a sacred part of the weave that makes up and completes the many Universes. We participate with all of those communities, which exist within this structure. This God consciousness weave is likened to a live webbing of fluid light that exists and touches all life force with its purity of love consciousness. This webbing plays the role as the Holy Connector within the Universes.

We need to understand that, yes, we are on Earth. Yes, we have begun to align to some essential aspects of our Higher Self. And we have our spiritual heritage connection that is held within the webbing that weaves throughout the many existing Universes. As we acknowledge the existence of the Universes we begin to naturally realign further into our higher purpose connection to that spiritual heritage.

Let's look at the complete picture of who we are within that extended multidimensional makeup within the whole. The action of the energy of the webbing is designed to support us in this New Dawning era for the accessing of our extended heritage. Our personal conscious connection within the Universe heralds in our transformation of the Collective Consciousness and this supports the ongoing awakening of humankind and impacts strongly our resident Universe.

As we begin to open into a fuller concept of our true place within the webbing we can discover how we move and operate within the relationship to these Universes. This sets in motion a deepening awareness of our higher nature, birthing a further initiation process within us. We will be drawn forward into the webbing, like a current in a river, to engage through the aspect of holiness that reflects through this frequency form connection. This action of the flow bathes us and we are absorbed into our spiritual heritage essence energy that exists, that is held within the Platform being maintained within the Collective Universes.

As we are rejoined to this Platform and begin these reconnections we become aware of being aligned to a different energetic rhythm, almost a hum. This hum will be absorbed into us, opening a sacred light connection into our cells, creating an organic interconnection through us, to the webbing. As this metamorphosis takes place there will be a compelling need within to let go as we are engulfed and realigned to these pure aspects of our heritage energy.

Our awareness will be magnified as we align to expanded dimensional levels of our higher-level existence. Another State of Self will be revealed to us. Through our willingness to allow this rebirth we will be compelled to let go, and we will perceive how we have become the inner hum. Within this action we are actually being received by our own Higher Selves within this Platform held within the Universes.

The God Seat of Power exists at the multidimensional Core held within the Collective Universes. This God Seat uses the form of the webbing to interact through the Collective Community and is responsible for holding a steady, pure frequency of light consciousness throughout all the Universes. This all-encompassing consciousness of the God Seat of Power manifests its own golden current of creation energy that flows through the structure of the webbing. The pure life force God Consciousness is interwoven within the webbing and radiates outward an echo that creates a synergy between all life force within the Collective Universes.

This echo will transmit the form of a pulsating light that will emanate directly through the God Seat of Power. This light will infiltrate, opening like a ray of brilliance flowing into the consciousness of all life force groups throughout the Universes. These are sacred transmissions that will create an illumination of the divine expression throughout the Universes. This action will expand and open up the unique God Consciousness state throughout, to all conscious beings. This life force will ripple outward and is designed to touch the very depth of the Home Space of humanity, aligning our Community to the Collective. This is the plan as we transition and unfold.

The Central Sun is the sacred light that synergizes with the God Seat of Power. The rays of the Central Sun infiltrate all the Universes, shining a brilliant vibrancy of enlightenment that manifests a natural sacred communion connection. Know that the God Seat of Power contains the full ascension knowledge of all multidimensional layers of existence.

We are to become a natural, interconnected part of this sacred synergy formed by the God Seat of Power and the Central Sun. Our full heritage frequency is carried within the force of this alliance. As we unfold, planet Earth will gain an energetic access into the Central Sun's direct pathway of consciousness. As we continue to unfold, we will begin to embody this sacred frequency, carrying our own unique brilliant link to the Central Sun. We are destined to play an extended role within our Universe as we embrace and become part of the sacred synergy with the God Seat and the Central Sun.

We are spiritual beings designed to evolve and continue to build and transform our communion connection. We have an unlimited capacity to flourish within our natural sacred heritage. Within our sacred heart cells, our Home Space, we have a dynamic geometrical form that holds the holy design of the God Seat of Power. Our sacred heritage is held in partnership within the God Seat. The God Seat oversees the completion energies of life within every form of consciousness, and this conscious form is an all-knowing, all-seeing expression of love that permeates through a timeless, limitless space of existence. We are part of this divine expression. This is our spiritual heritage. Our enlightenment involves opening a doorway into the space of knowing, and then moving into the direct experience of our unlimited form. Through our spiritual heritage we will have this interaction of communion to the God Seat.

We already have forged an opening with the God Seat with what the Pleiadians call the Sacred Trust. Once this Sacred Trust has been made manifest through our initiations with the Keys, this natural reconnection remains impeccably authentic for all time. Once established, this sacred connection formed by the Sacred Trust will continue to evolve, ever flowing through our Home Space, through our heritage imprint, outwards, and aligning to the Platform held within the Universes.

We will open into an ever-growing awareness of levels that exist within these Collective Universes, and we will unfold further into these new vistas. Simultaneously we will meet the unfolding layers, which is the sacred within us. The Universes exist and we exist within this sacred imprint of the "knowing." As we become more cognizant of our sacred existence and are willing to acknowledge that which we are, we naturally begin to channel this expansive unlimited, multidimensional world through the Sacred Trust within our Home space.

Our connection to the Sacred Trust is forged through our inner torch, which is a unique relationship between us, the God Seat, and Central Sun. A signature consciousness is formed through this combined synergy, and is anchored by the God Seat. This energetic bond design will link our Higher Self consciousness into our physical cells. There will be a heightened awareness through our Home Space that will develop, like a sixth sense. The Sacred Trust will hold the design as part of a bridge from the God Seat to develop our Higher Self senses, transforming our heart cells to enable us to evolve into the higher Universal Consciousness Realms of our sacred heritage.

The Central Sun's rays move with a strong purpose, as the rays align through the heavenly bodies and onto Earth. The rays use our Sacred Trust within our Home Space to channel their energy. We each hold a unique connection frequency to the Central Sun within us that will expand within our Sacred Trust bridge connection.

The design of our Sacred Trust has the ability to create a mirroring that reflects the full capacity of our heritage within our multidimensional Home Space. This action opens us up to fulfill our role within the entire Universal Community by expanding our individual connections to the God Seat. This mirroring is designed to enable us to open into the full picture of our sacred heritage and to consciously explore who we are within the wholeness of the sacred that exists within our own resident Universe.

A significant aspect of this path right now is the need to receive the energy of Truth, and open into what is right in front of us within the moment. It is the time for us to open to this deepening of understanding of who we are and begin to unfold into this new level of spiritual maturity. So that we can begin to move through this Truth and embrace where we fit within this larger picture. Where do we belong within the full essence of these Collective Universes? What are our individual and collective roles that we are destined to play within these arenas? We need to ask ourselves these questions.

Each one of us is being called to acknowledge our heritage within the Universes. This acknowledgment is key to our enlightenment process, and we need to move quickly to anchor our energetic reality settings that exist within the Platform held within the Universes. We must return to these sacred aspects of Self, aligning through the multidimensional doorways that give us access to our complete heritage. This conscious action by us begins to form the completion energy within our resident Universe.

Know that at this juncture of our mission the focused intent needs to be predominately held within our own resident Universe. We will be received and be given orientation to what we are to accomplish, and where we are needed within our Universal connections. As we begin to embark, through this acknowledgment of our own heritage within the Collective Universes, there will be clarity, a remembering process activated.

Our mission will be unveiled and the forming of important alliances will take place for us to fulfill our roles. We will not be alone. We will be part of a conscious unit made up from the different life force groups within our resident Universe. And this includes other human beings on planet Earth.

Know that there are many heavenly bodies that exist within the different dimensional settings within our own Universe and surrounding our planet. These heavenly bodies carry different dimensional layers that play a major role in contributing to the changing energies on our planet. Each individual heavenly body contains a variation of divine light settings that we can draw upon as we become consciously aligned to our Universal connections.

These specific settings that are held within the different vibrational heavenly bodies hold unique dimensional alignments that interact with the human consciousness. Many of us on the earth plane have strong pre-agreement ties to the Angels, and they are part of the Universal team supporting humankind during this transition on Earth. Through these specific settings that they hold, there are unique reawakening energies to support those of us on the path that are the "way showers." They bring guidance, and move us through into a deeper and more profound transformational state of consciousness with them. They act as leaders, lighting the path for us to follow as we reconnect to the webbing that interconnects us and aligns us, supporting our mission of completion with our resident Universe.

Through our reemergence of interaction with the heavenly bodies there is a specific angelic pulsation, that opens an original imprinting, that naturally enters our sacred heritage energies. This imprinting is mirrored, creating newly designed light settings that transfer through our physical body and create an evolving expansion of our energetic centers. These imprints are designed to support our ongoing energetic transformational work with our own resident Universe and will open an awareness of the Platform held by the Universes.

We will enter a new phase of our development, consciously being able to multiplex within multidimensional settings. This ability will bring us into being aware of many openings simultaneously and to be able to interact with many facets of energies at the same time. This is a common ability as you initiate into the Higher Realms.

These changes within us open our ability to function within the Platform held by the God Seat. This shift will move us into a more fluid state, allowing us to flow effortlessly through the different energetic interactions. It's as though we will become like an energetic ripple that moves through the webbing connection.

Our awakened signature, in the form of heritage ripples, contributes to the re-opening of a multidimensional doorway within the home sphere of our resident Universe. Through this opening our Universe will move into a more direct alignment to the Central Sun and the God Seat of Power. This will create a repositioning of our entire resident Universe, bringing us into a more complete alignment within the Universes. This is an aspect of the goal.

There is a lot of networking necessary for us participate within the Universe. Part of our mission is to begin a conscious collective communion within our own Universe. We need to learn how to develop new relationships within our own neighborhood, within our resident Universe. It is important for each one of us to develop an understanding and appreciation of the importance of this networking process. We are a representative group for planet Earth. We are to play the role of Ambassadors and we do this on behalf of humankind. Know the importance of our individual and collective group roles as we open our awareness and interact consciously within these multidimensional realms of life force groups that live within our Universe. We are part of this Community.

We need to turn toward our Universe and this is achieved through our conscious interaction with the life force groups that exist here. We have an essential responsibility to work within the Universal Community, to build alliances with them. This link is created from our God Consciousness, Oneness connection, which makes this networking possible on many levels because we can come together through that collective communion link. These reconnections are needed for us to fulfill our mission here within our own Universe.

I have discussed this process in earlier chapters of this book. Now we are looking at the importance of Community Connections for the evolution of our own Universe.

The focus within our Universe has been on our planet Earth's evolution. This is a Truth. We strongly impact the Universal energies as we transform dimensionally here on the earth plane. There is a great importance for our own Universe to evolve on yet another level, and as Earth transforms, we bring a completion to our local Universe. Through this completion we can then, as a Universe, begin to align more fully to the Central Sun and to the God Seat of Power. These higher interactions will open an entry point for us as a Universe to join the Collective Universes. We will carry this higher frequency of light within the dimensional layers of interaction to all life force that exists within our realm. This higher light will operate within our entire resident Universe. There will be an expansion of divine content birth from the God Seat and flow through the consciousness of all life force groups within our Universe.

Now we can begin to understand why the entire Universe is focused on our planet Earth and is so strongly invested in supporting us in our transition. Those of us on Earth and all the life force groups within the Universe have a commonality, a goal. We are all interconnected in this mission to deepen our alignment to the Central Sun and the God Seat of Power for our ongoing awakening as a Collective Consciousness Group returning to the Collective Universes. We can begin to appreciate more fully how we are on this collective mission within our Universe.

Our vision has been limited through the illusion here on Earth, but now we begin to know and understand the bigger picture. We need to come together holding a united vision knowing the essential role that we play here on the planet and within our Universe. It is time for us to take ownership of our place within our resident Universe, so we can align and participate fully in a different way, in a much more conscious way.

I know when this information was imparted to me, I became excited. I suddenly understood aspects of what I had been participating in for so long. To finally understand the full part of my mission was so refreshing. I felt as though I had been gifted with a complete picture, which gave me a greater focus to work as a team member with humanity and with the many life force groups that make up our resident Universe. This made so much sense and answered so many of my questions. The clarity allowed me to move forward and bring myself into my role with joy and a new purpose.

I found I was no longer holding back any part of myself and I could receive the support that was being offered to me in a new light. Before I had not understood why so much help was being offered, and this question impacted my ability to fully receive and fully engage with the Universal Community. I realized that I held the Universal Community in a separate state from me on a subtle level. Now I was able to let go and allow the Community energy in on a very different level than ever before because I understood the bigger picture of which I was a part.

This unfolding is a sacred fulfillment that is part of our destiny bringing us into an understanding of the full Community that exists, that we are each a part of. We can now truly let go and open up to the expansive energy of our Family of Light consciousness. We can begin a deeper appreciation of the network of light that has always existed and that we have always been held within this weave. Through this wholeness, we can claim our collective essence. This is simply who we are; we are who we have been waiting for.

Know how essential it is for us to rest in this knowledge, to truly let go and allow these divine Truths to digest, nourish, and embrace us. We can let go and just relax, knowing that we are being held within this collective framework, by our expanded being of our Higher Self. We can let go within this Truth. We can breathe and feel our self being fully received by our collective Self that exists within the multidimensional Universes within the Platform. We are coming home!

As we unfold into our new relationship within the Universe we will expand our relationship to the Angelic Realms and work consciously through the different settings held within these heavenly bodies. Our transformation allows us to move more fluidly, energetically throughout the Universe. As we take a fuller role within our place we align to the new components that exist on that multidimensional level within our space of the webbing that embodies our heritage. Opening us into a more profound, natural, and innate understanding of who we are in reality, in relationship to the goals that are set within our resident Universe.

We will be restored to enter our Universal World fully as we become part of our own multidimensional setting within the Universe. There is an immersion by the Central Sun that will unfold within us because of our alignment to the Sacred Trust in our heart cells. It is designed to support a reopening to the many reconnections, to the different life force groups that exist within our Universe. This interaction with the Central Sun will accelerate our mission of re-entering the Central Platform held within the Universes as we are moved within the higher communion states that exist there.

As we merge into these higher communion states we will become aware of the heavenly body that exists. Through this communion, we can accelerate our ability in fulfilling our role, as a "way shower" on Earth. By choosing to take our place consciously within this Universe, we will experience the building of the sacred that we are. As we develop a more complete union we will enter a metamorphic process and our altered state will give us the ability to interact through a communion setting with the rest of the Universes.

Through our Sacred Trust connection, we are able to first perceive the collective Universes and then open into the Time Line spaces held between the Universes. There is a woven network between the Universes within the Time Line spaces. As we become reinstated consciously through this network we will begin to recollect multidimensional aspects of Self. This meeting point that contains the Time Line space interacts fully within our sacred heritage. This is a space that exists beyond and through all time, where we are held within "the moment" where all unfolding takes place ultimately for every life force individual with the Universes. They are waiting for us to choose, to make our way back to Home Base, to Self.

As we fulfill our heritage alliances back to Home through the Universes, our connection to the Central Sun and the God Seat of Power will evolve, and we will begin to engage through our new dimensional vistas. As we take a more active role within our Universe we can begin to meet ourselves on an accelerated level of Self.

Sacred times will continue to prevail as we commit to our ongoing profound unfolding, gaining a new level of growth within our spiritual evolution. Some of our unraveling entails new revelations through the dynamics that exist within this Universe and the energetic connections that arise from the other Universes. We will continue to open into a deepening maturity as we build our understanding of these truths and begin to integrate the essences of this sacred communion that simply resides within us on a multidimensional level.

We have two powerful energetic Suns that are strongly impacting our New Dawning era. They are designed to play a dynamic role by joining in a sacred synergy, bathing the earth plane with a pure force of light and expanding the sacred that is held within the Central Platform of the Universes.

It is important to establish a distinction between our Sun on planet Earth and the Central Sun that exists within the Universes. The Sun on our planet supports an integration process within us as we awaken. It provides nourishment for us by carrying an aspect of dimensional light consciousness for the awakening of the physical cells in our body, and it holds the energetic imprint of this New Dawning evolution on our planet.

The Sun's rays are working through the natural forces, bringing an expansion of consciousness. The energy held within these rays is realigning nature back to its original Blueprint form, realigning nature back to its pristine state. Our Sun is playing an essential role by reopening the dimensional energetic settings within nature and reopening the creation energies within the Earth's Core. The Sun is interacting through newly activated Portals, vortexes, and ley lines that are instrumental in the transformation on our planet.

As we re-establish our sacred connection to the Central Sun there is a destiny that opens between our Sun on planet Earth and the Central Sun. Collectively they are destined to bring a transformational frequency on our planet within the moment. At that sacred time there will be an acceleration of the God Seat of Power flowing throughout our planet. This will occur when our resident Universe is complete and returns fully to align to the God Seat within the very Central Platform of the Universes. This anchoring will re-establish the light of the Central Sun channeling through our Sacred Trust, and then it aligns naturally onto our planet. This will touch the consciousness of humanity, creating miraculous healing on many levels through humankind. We will experience the building of the sacred that we are through the deepening of this union.

The God Seat of Power has begun a series of specific transmissions to awaken those of us who are ready. This energy from the God Seat transmits a subtle blending of light that moves through the heavenly bodies and throughout planet Earth. This is where we are now in our evolution. We will complete our mission successfully in this lifetime.

A Sacred Trust patterning is designed to enable you to forge a sacred synergy with the Sacred Sun, the God Seat of Power, and the Sacred Trust within your Home Space. These higher forms will propel you forward into a more expanded initiation state of your heritage. This will enable you to interact on a higher level with the Central Sun, and deepen your Sacred Trust with the God Seat of Power. There will be a strong need to let go as you work, being willing to allow a full reconfiguration within you to open up. There is no need to hold on any longer, simply Trust.

Note: You   can   find   an   audio   file   link   at *www.christinedayonline.com/pleiadianpromise*

1. Activate your Sacred Trust—Sound: EE...STAE (page 143)

This will be a simple process of listening to the audio file, and letting go as you work within the Sacred Trust patterning that is given to you. You will always have your pattern in front of you when you work with the audio file.

The audio file is designed as a multidimensional document, which means that each time you take the journey it will be different. Each time you listen to the audio file you will access higher frequencies of your natural heritage. Each time you listen to the audio file you will be carrying a higher frequency of Self.

The initiation energies are unlimited and so are you!

Sacred Trust

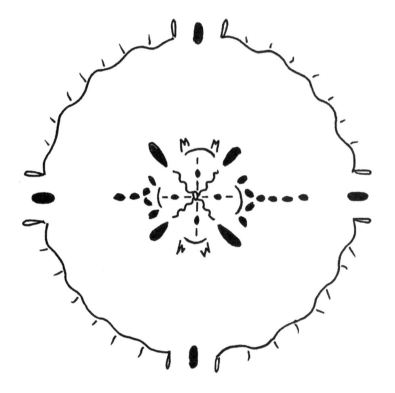

Sound: EE... STAE

Chapter 9
Open to the Timeline

One of the biggest illusions on our earth plane is the concept of time. As a human race we have a complete involvement with this illusion, the existence of time. We are preoccupied with and affected by time every waking moment of our day. The general consensus is that we do not have enough time to complete what we have to do. We are continuously in a race with the clock.

We are pressured by this illusion of time and we are limited by time restraints on any given day. Time is always factored into every experience and decision-making process. Time controls our thought process and restricts our movements. Our whole life is broken down into segments of time. Our ego mind is constantly aware of what time it is now. The illusion around time keeps us in a perpetual cycle of running from one thing to the next, often anxious that we may be late or that we might miss out on something important.

Our entire planet is completely run from the perspective that time actually exists. We, as a human race, are strongly anchored within this illusion as a group. As a collective consciousness we forge this patterning between us that creates an iron grip to hold this illusion in place. There is the creation of a continual drama around the elements associated with time in our lives.

This concept of time keeps us in a limited, contained space that breaks down our full potential. Time creates a strong separating element from Truth because Truth cannot exist within illusion. The ego mind takes hold of this concept and is in continuous dialogue regarding being productive, doing the right thing at the right time, prioritizing, making lists, getting things done, and the central theme to all of this is time.

As we strongly engage with this belief system we completely separate out from our authentic nature and so there is a breakdown of real intimacy with others. We are disconnected from the intuitive aspect of ourselves and become disengaged from what is fully possible. Through this separation we lose our spontaneity and become leaden, robotic-like, as we live out this limitation and illusion of our lives through the constraints of time.

There can be no freedom to experience ourselves within our life under this dictatorship, which is ruled by our ego mind over the issue of time. We are pushed to move faster to get through the restrictions that time perpetuates. There is no true fulfillment, as we are taken away from anything that is spontaneously free flowing and natural within our own multidimensionality.

Through a shifting awareness of our focus we will return into our natural essence. Finally, through our awareness of time as illusion we are moved beyond the separated state. As we breathe into the energy we hold around time we begin to break down the patterned imprint, which has been forged on Earth. We loosen these bonds created by our collective group mentality, releasing the illusion, the belief, and allow a new flow of liberation to open up through us.

Within the rest of the Universe and through all multidimensional settings the frequency of time does not exist. As we let go, rejoining the Universal Community, we enter this limitless free-flowing element within that brings us into a thriving existence. Within this flow is our ability to align to our natural rhythm for manifestation, for a deep unfolding our own uniqueness to be, a freedom of expression and joy. Within this flow there is a huge space for the natural movement of the individual expression of our own magic.

Moving past this concept of time means we need to let go and trust an aspect of the unlimited consciousness that exists within the Universe. Remember: We are an essential aspect of that unlimited force. As we choose to move beyond this aspect of illusion, a veil can lift and we are led into a new experience of being within "the multidimensional moment." This is an endless, unlimited space. This alternative space receives the design of our own consciousness that allows the full expression and operation of our own multidimensionality.

The Pleiadians refer to what exists outside this illusion of time as the Timeless space.

As we choose to move beyond this illusion we are able to re-enter this unlimited space, which moves and aligns us to our full creative energy. This Timeless space is an interconnected aspect that allows us a freedom of simply Being, free flowing into an unlimited experience of creativity. Within this multidimensional flowing space, which exists in reality within our Universe and within us, we can truly open to our natural unique expression.

Within the Timeless space we will function through a different dimensional setting that naturally operates within us because we will not be hampered by illusion. We will move beyond the constraints that block our real Self. Within this space we each have within our multidimensional makeup an inbuilt timer that sources directly from our Higher Self. We function through an intuitive, unlimited form that is an aspect of the flow within the multidimensional world. This sacred form of Self exists and sources through our Home Space within our heart.

This Timeless space connects us to the full multidimensional potential within every moment. The space within the moment opens up and provides an energetic arena that can hold every experience in its fullest state. This means that every possible dimensional component within every experience is accessible to complete us, bringing the design of Truth for us to continually receive.

As multidimensional beings, we are able to naturally access the multidimensional states that reside within this Timeless space. We are able to return back into any one moment and reconnect to any experience we have had from the past. Because there is no such thing as time we can return to any individual experience and link into the unlimited potential of what truly exists within that experience. This link allows us to open up and receive the richness of the many dimensional layers that make up a full experience. We can re-access our unique experience any number of times through the Timeless space. This enables us to unveil and digest the full multidimensional elements that occurred at the time of our initial experience.

Typically, we are unable to fully utilize or appreciate the full potential in the moment an experience takes place. The ego mind often interrupts by bringing in dialogue about what we should be doing instead, or breaking down our experience in some way, which stops us from fully embracing all that is presenting in "the unlimited moment."

Re-accessing the moment is valuable because it enables us to fully take in and absorb what is still there for us to receive from that past experience. This reconnection to previous events opens up the opportunity for us to receive the complete teaching energy that is being held within the experience. This gives us time to digest the fullness of the energy, which was anchored, and most importantly being presented in the moment, within the experience.

Another essential element of this process is that we can revisit and open to higher levels of energy that existed in the moment we were having our experience. Understand that every experience we have is set in an energetic multidimensional form.

Let's be clear about what is meant by multidimensional form. When I talk about a multidimensional energy, I am referring to the fact that there is a layered vibrational light that exists within every dimensional energetic experience. We can always return to an experience and open into another energetic layer of that experience when we are ready. This means that we can receive one level of light from the experience within the energy and know that there are many other, higher layers of light for us to engage with and integrate. Or levels of knowledge or of understanding held within the experience to receive. Everything has an unlimited form within an experience that we can tap into again and again.

Let me give you an example of the multidimensionality existing within an energetic experience. Let's say there are ten energetic levels of light held within an energetic experience. At the moment of the experience we receive maybe three of those energetic levels. There are seven of those energetic levels of energy we are not ready to receive yet. We can't take them in because they may hold too high a vibrational light for us to access at that moment. Maybe we are not ready to integrate them, or maybe the ego mind distracted us in that moment. So we integrate and receive the energy of just three of those levels.

When we are ready to receive more, we can return back to "the moment" of that experience, which still exists and is waiting for us in the Timeless space. As we re-enter the experience we can meet and connect to more of the energetic levels. We can receive more levels because we are holding a higher vibration now within our body through the integration from those first three levels from our initial experience. We may then be able to take in all the other seven levels of the energy that were contained within the energetic experience and integrate them. We have now received all of those 10 levels of energy within the experience that are uniquely ours for our ongoing awakening process. We can always return to the moment as many times as we need to integrate the energy held within any one experience.

Sometimes we may have an interaction with a Being of Light in an experience. We can return to the moment and take in more of the communion energy that existed between us, and that Being of Light, taking in more of the pure love that existed within that experience. We can continually return within this Timeless space for reconnection and absorption of further levels of higher frequencies.

You may find you are having a profound experience in a group meditation or receiving a powerful transmission from a Master on this planet. You can move into the Timeless space and reconnect to this experience taking in yet another form of the light frequency that was being transmitted that event. This can be the next day or months later—it does not matter, because the moment exists within the Timeless space forever.

This is the meaning of multidimensionality, that there are many individual energetic experiences contained within the one experience. We can always return to any energetic experience and open to receive another level through that experience. It is possible for us to operate within these expanded experiences from the past because we are in reality a multidimensional being. There is no limitation in utilizing the Timeless space. Each time we enter this multidimensional setting we realign to another form of our own multidimensionality. This reconnection is accumulative through our physical cells. Every time we work within this format we naturally awaken and embody our own multidimensionality more and more. This is an unlimited natural aspect of our makeup.

Remember: We are multidimensional spiritual beings having a human experience. We have spent lifetimes having our human experience and evolving through these third-dimensional dynamics. In this lifetime we have come to the point of moving from one phase of our journey of originally evolving through having our human experience, to a next step phase of experiencing our spiritual multidimensionality while still in our human form. We have reached this next step and this is exciting!

We begin to shift and accelerate in our awakening, because our reason for being here has changed. Now is the time for us to open and utilize our multidimensional natures. We need to realize and recognize our own unique multidimensional potential. We will begin to open into our multidimensionality by working in the Timeless space.

Let's look at the process that will move you back into a past energetic experience. Opening up to the Truth that there is no such thing as time, you will understand that whether your experience was yesterday or two years ago is immaterial. Your experience still exists.

You move back into the energy of the experience by opening your awareness into an aspect of the experience that you recall. For example, it may be an emotion that comes to you, which may be sensory—a feeling or a visual. One aspect of the experience is not more than another. What is important is that you choose what still impacts you within your memory from that past experience. This is what I call your link to the experience.

Begin to focus in on that link, bringing your awareness into the focused aspect of that link. Bring your awareness to the link—feeling, sensing, seeing—and use your Conscious Breath. Place your breath, like a soft wind, directly into that link—that aspect of your experience. As you do this, the energy may grow in some way within your link. It may expand or a further experience may be felt or sensed, or you may see something newly formed.

You need to follow the growing experience once more with your awareness. Use the breath again, directing it into the experience. You may feel yourself being drawn deeper into the experience. Keep letting go and using the Conscious Breath, bringing your awareness into what is presenting or opening up. You may feel a deepening of that experience open further, interacting with you. As you place the breath into the energy of the experience again you are automatically taken back into a fuller moment of the energetic experience. Know that you are actively opening up into the multidimensional layers held within your experience. You will be receiving, in some way, further levels of that experience.

You may be surprised what unfolds within this individual expression of the experience. What is essential is to be with whatever is presenting in the moment and not to allow the ego mind to comment, break down or manipulate the experience. It is essential to keep letting go into the experience while you open to the fullness and vastness of each expression as it unfolds. Working this way gives you an opportunity to open up into the experience more completely, and take in more of the energetic flow around the experience than you were able to allow previously.

As we work within this aspect of the Timeless space we can begin to develop our natural ability to move through different dimensional states effortlessly. This is what we are actually doing within this process. We are choosing consciously to utilize our own ability to work within the different dimensional network spaces within our experience. This is an important stepping-stone, a self-empowering action. We get to fully comprehend "the moment" and reclaim our own multidimensional connection to the Timeless space that we are aligning through, as we work within our experience.

Witness how, as we align to the Timeless space, we will begin to find a common vibrational light connection that exists between our own multidimensional energy and the Timeless space. This connection anchors and stabilizes us within the dimensional energetic framework patterns that exist within the full Timeless space, which exists throughout the Universes. Remember that we are not separate from any energetic light pattern. We are interconnected to all energetic patterns that naturally exist within the Collective Universes. This connection is made possible because of our own multidimensional form.

The Pleiadians talk about accessing a further space that resides within this Timeless space, which they call the Timeline. This Timeline makes up an aspect of the Timeless space, and holds a higher frequency flow than the Timeless space. The Timeline has a very different functionality than the Timeless space. They are not separate, just different forms interrelating to each other within a multidimensional space. We are aligned naturally to both spaces through our own multidimensional nature.

This Timeline has always been, arising and existing within the pure fluidity from the Timeless space within the Collective Universes. The Timeline holds a powerful seat within the Central Platform, which carries a sacred form of alignment originating within the Universes. The combined synergy of consciousness of the God Seat of Power and Central Sun oversee the complete frequency network that makes up the full Timeline structure. Remember: We are interconnected with this synergy through our Home Space, which allows us to work within the Timeline effectively as we are held by the constructed Platform.

In Truth, all experiences are held within one framework moment within the Timeline. We can access future and past and present experiences within the moment. This allows us to reconnect to past and future energetic events within the Timeline. Each one of us is linked within the frequency network within the Timeline that flows like webbing throughout the Universes. Through our own multidimensional nature, we are an aspect of this network, which allows us to enter the Timeline flow.

We carry our own multidimensional signature within us that is recognized within the Timeline, and we can interact freely within the Timeline flow. Our unique signature will provide our sacred co-ordinates through the Timeline. With these unique coordinates we will be able to navigate through the multidimensional spaces. Here we recollect that which we are ready to utilize now in our life. As we realign to past or future energies, we integrate and upload these through our energetic field.

The Timeline carries all the encompassing frequency of existence, which has always been within the Universes. This profound flowing light current is a multidimensional flow and is completely electrical in nature. The Timeline is made up of a series of network pathways that work throughout the Platforms that are held within the Universes. These pathways flow through all time continuums simultaneously, which allow us to free flow within the full network of the Timeline.

We all enter the Timeline through conscious choice, choosing to let go and allowing our experience, knowing that we will be taken through our sacred coordinates to where we need to be placed for our next step. This Timeline is being made available to us now for the sole purpose of moving us consciously toward the direct experience of our spiritual signatures.

The Timeline has many functions and we will become aware of those as we embark and grow into our own multidimensionality and mature through our awakening processes. The Timeline has its own consciousness state, which cannot be manipulated, controlled, or corrupted for any negative purpose. It holds the purest frequency of light and a higher purpose for the good of all that enter.

Let's begin to open into the steps that will take us on our Timeline journey. This is a simple process. Remember: We each hold our multidimensional signature energy within us that contains the frequency settings for us to naturally fit within the energy of the Timeline structure. Through our signature we are placed on a specific network within the Timeline to reconnect to some sacred aspects of Self. Or possibly to receive tools that belong to us from the past or future times that we are now ready to utilize to support us in the completion of our missions. All energies that we encounter within the Timeline are aspects of our higher nature. There is nothing that we can meet that is not of the highest light vibration, as only the purest forms exist within the Timeline space.

To enter the Timeline flow you will work with the Timeline Template Columns (see the diagram on page 156). As you learn to align with the Template Columns through the help of the audio file you will enter the Timeline flow effortlessly. As you get familiar with the entry process through the Columns you will not necessarily need to use the audio file. You will discover that you can easily enter the Timeline on your own, by simply utilizing the Template Columns.

The Pleiadians give this sacred sound, ASKE STAH, to enter the Timeline flow. As you utilize this sound you will create your unique frequency that forms a synergy between your own multidimensional signature and the Timeline flow. You will be moved into the flow and energetically positioned to a specific multidimensional time link into the past or future energetic setting that you need for your next step of this journey. Here you will be reconnected through an initiation, then integrated and aligned to this energetic form that exists.

You will be reconnecting to a Sacred Realm aspect of your Higher Self through these individual positions within the Timeline flow.

Let's look at how you will access and manage the specific form of reconnection to these energies as you encounter them within the Timeline. I liken these encounters on your Timeline position to receiving a wrapped gift. For example, you may encounter this energetic form, which may be presented as the energy of peace, or a brilliant light, or even a physical geometrical form or a sound.

Whatever your experience happens to be, you need to bring your full awareness into meeting what is there that you are experiencing in "the moment." Open up into what you encounter as you bring your conscious awareness into the experience. You bring your Conscious Breath, like a soft wind, and place it within the space and let go. This allows you to establish an alignment through the energy of the form, claiming ownership.

Now you need to take the wrapping off the gift. There is no point in aligning to this energy and not fully receiving what is yours. For example, if you have a geometrical form within this space, you may see, sense, or feel this form. This is an energetic tool that you are reconnecting to so that you can utilize it in your life now. To access and realign to the full energy of this gift, you bring your awareness into the tool (in this example, the geometrical form). You begin to bring your Conscious Breath, like a soft wind, into the tool. This breath takes you deeper within the experience, and you will begin to experience the energy within the tool beginning to open up and merge within you. It may possibly transmit its frequency into you. The form of the geometrical shape may change or dissolve as you open into the multifaceted aspects held within the tool. You continue to unwrap aspects of your gift with your awareness and breath until you have forged a complete ownership, a total alignment with the energy of the tool through you.

Once you have completed this reclaiming of your energy from the form through you, return back to the Template Columns. You will find that your Higher Self energy will bring you naturally back to this point on the Timeline at which you started your journey. Remember that this is your own multidimensional aspect working with you in this recovery process.

This is how your own unique Timeline works.

We get to unfold ourselves within the Timeline. Each journey is individual, and there is a need to allow a full integration between each Timeline journey. As we go through these individual initiations within the Timeline we will go through an accelerated metamorphic process within. Our DNA strands will go through a repositioning process as we recollect these sacred energetic pockets and realign them through our system. As we align further within our own natural state of multidimensionality, we need to continue letting go and give ourselves the moments to Be after each journey.

Just know how amazing and imperative these Timeline journeys will become for you. There are powerful adjustments that take place within us on a multidimensional level each time we take a journey through the flow. As I journeyed through my Timeline, I began to move into a new level of clarity as I recollected energy from my past, as I assimilated the tools that I needed now from my future.

We are moving so quickly into our awakening process that we are requiring the access to these energetic tools now. The Timeline is very necessary for many of us so that we can propel ourselves forward into our enlightenment, opening up a path for all of humankind, and entering into a completion cycle within our resident Universe.

The Pleiadians and all the Galactic Community alongside the Angelic Realms are with us while we unfold into this powerful rebirthing process. Mother Mary and the Christ energy support us in our integration processes, as we transform.

Note: You can find an audio file link at *www.christinedayonline.com/pleiadianpromise*

You will listen to the audio file and work with your Timeline Template page.

Enjoy the journey!

Timeline Template

Sound: ASKE STAH

Chapter 10

The Space Beyond Reason

Shafts of light begin to flow directly from the Collective space held between the Universes, the light pulsating its brilliance through all time continuums, sending forth the purest form of frequency, presenting as an echo of blue, golden light moving outward. This perfect form of consciousness returns as a gift from our sacred presence back to us, unveiling an innocence that is held within the opening of our light form.

Suddenly there is a bursting, a brilliant explosion of this energetic form of liquid light that carries the full expression of Truth that exists as the full expression of Self. This pure force of consciousness arises from a series of our sacred Overlays. They contain the design of creation, expanding and building as they gather momentum. Opening further, revealing the true essence of our multidimensional selves that exist, simultaneously, moving together in a sacred synergy through the parallel Universes.

These series of Overlays hold the mirror of the enormous potential of our fully enlightened Higher Self. They carry the complete and complex expression of our existence. They are the combined force of our interwoven state within the Collective Universes. Within the weave is are our natural state of being. We embody the unlimited ongoing creation that exists within us, emanating the light, which is continually gathering momentum.

These series of sacred Overlays of light are the backdrop to a pure consciousness state. They are the full expression of us being the God Seat of Power from which we have all arisen and are a part, and we are destined to return to Self within this space. Our time has come; we are being carried by this current as we are being realigned back Home.

This blue, golden light consciousness is interwoven through the heart, the Home Space, and links through our brain. It moves within every multidimensional aspect of our consciousness within the parallel Universes. This is the divine connection of the One, originating through us and interconnecting us to every living organism within the Collective Universes.

We are made up as an aspect of this super structure, and we carry the frequency of this blue, golden aura within our multidimensional heart and Home Space. Our aura interconnects us to "the space beyond reason," which holds our multifaceted aspect of our paralleled lives within other Universes that we exist within. This space beyond reason has been outside our realm to be able to consciously process and has not been able to function energetically within us until now. We are being gifted with the access to this space, which the Higher Realm aspects of our Self have inhabited for lifetimes. We are now able to reach the sacred components of our Higher Self through our connection within this blue, golden frequency. This fusion allows us to move beyond what we have known and to reach through the expanded consciousness of the Collective of which we are a part.

Within these Collective Universes a space is being held for us that carries elements of profound understanding of the Promise energy. There is currently a doorway that has opened that holds revelations of this alternate reality of Truth for us to digest. Now is our time to move through this doorway and investigate our heritage states, which will allow us to open into a further exposure to Truth that provides the Knowledge to assist us in our Homecoming.

The Pleiadians suggest that we make a decision not to try to understand what these Truths contain, but rather to choose to let go and absorb the energy they contain, allowing our Conscious Breath to do its job of realigning us naturally to these Truths.

The Pleiadians speak of the frequency created by the use of the three Conscious Breaths that will begin to open us up to access another level of our senses. These three Conscious Breaths will energetically align us to our multidimensional settings where the blue, golden frequency is woven within our brain and heart Home Space. These combined breaths open us to a new seventh sense of knowing. This will enable us to work with the multidimensional series of Overlays that exist in our parallel lives, and within the multidimensional states within the Collective Universes.

We have lived here on our earth plane having our human experience, and simultaneously we have coexisted in other parallel Universes through our series of Overlays. An Overlay is a higher, more evolved aspect of us that exists in a parallel universe where we are interconnected with an advanced Higher Realm aspect of Self. This sacred connection flows within our heart, Home Space structure. Whether we are consciously aware of this or not is immaterial. We have always been aligned energetically with our Overlay parts.

We all have many Overlay aspects in existence and they are all set in different parallel Universes in various stages of evolution. Through this multidimensional setting they hold an energetic flow around us, bringing guidance in the form of an interaction with our intuition, which supports us in our missions here. We have been working hand-in-hand with our Overlays during our journey on this earth plane. We may not have been consciously aware of this working alliance; however, now is the time for us to let go into a rapid initiation by forming a conscious alliance and merging with our Overlays. This step allows an accelerated birthing process, through our alignment to the intricate patterns of creation that the Overlays individually carry.

There have been multidimensional connections that have been lying dormant within our heart, Home Space, and brain that are ready to be accessed, opened, and utilized by us. As we are brought into alignment through the blue, golden frequency settings, the connection to each one of our individual Overlays will be made possible.

Our alignment to these blue, golden frequency settings takes us through a doorway not previously accessible in this lifetime. This doorway opening will propel us into a different setting of reality judgment. As we unfold into this process our heart center, Home Space will access and understand a new purpose. We will be able to open and perceive a different reality that will bring us into profound clarity settings. This will allow us to witness and align to all that is significant for us to understand, and then lead us forth in our transition of awakening. Through our holding of this new perception of judgment we can then readily let go and align to the pure frequencies held within our individual Overlays, which exist in these alternate realities.

As we align we can be moved by our individual Overlays and discover a natural state of being that takes us beyond what we have previously known as reality. We are able to enter "the space beyond reason," which is an alternative existence within the blue, golden frequency Community anchored centrally within the Collective Universes.

Let's look at this interwoven energy that has been in existence for all time within the Collective frequency space. We examine Truth that is no longer being hidden from view, from us as a human group. There is an unveiling. This is a revolutionary event of our re-emergence into Community, which involves full disclosure from the Collective Community of the Universes to us on planet Earth. Knowledge is empowerment, and now is the time for us to be returned to the fold of the Community.

We are ready to grasp the full understanding within the true place that we hold through the dynamics of this Collective Community within the Universes. As we participate we are able to anchor all that will energetically unfold within as we align to our Overlays through this parallel universe setting. Through these energetic initiations we will be able to begin an adjustment period within ourselves, which will be specifically designed to enable us to consciously rejoin these alternate realities. To begin this conscious step is a destiny moment—to become once more a conscious part of the flow that these essential movements create, becoming part of a navigational current that exists within these parallel settings.

There are many realities taking place simultaneously within these parallel Universes. We are existing in all of these individual realities. Through the Timeline we are given access to these series of multidimensional living experiences. By being in the moment we can open consciously into these varied vibrational aspects of Self, playing our roles in different settings within the different worlds.

The Overlay aspects of ourselves are made up from the intricate patterns of life creation that interact constantly through the Oneness, the Collective God Consciousness. Energetically there always has been an interaction that has taken place between our Overlay aspects of Self and our human part. Our human aspect is generally unaware of the existence of our Overlay forms even though we have been consistently being held and supported through these Higher Realm Overlay aspects.

At this juncture in our evolution these Overlay aspects can begin to align with our human part and there are energetic pathways opening for us to follow. This is all being created through our own sacred Higher Realm design. These pathways are playing an essential role by creating light currents that are drawing us, like a magnet, to a correct positioned coordinate for the recalibration of our systems. These will align us to an individual Overlay that we are ready to initiate through. This deep transformation will allow us to be able to open consciously into this next phase of our evolution. The individual bonding process with aspects of our Overlay designs brings an accelerated level of awakened consciousness in the form of knowledge and clarity. This awakening opens up a pure form of communion for us.

We don't get to choose the Overlay aspect we blend with in the Timeline process. As we enter the Timeline our signature energy is aligned through the network to the correct Overlay form that we are ready to re-engage for our next step. As we interact through the Timeline a blending will occur with the Overlay aspects of Self. This enables us to re-emerge consciously, deepening the opening into our own unique weaving of light.

We begin to be fed directly from a higher knowledge multidimensional perspective through each unique Overlay design of our Higher Self. As we open into the experience from this powerful alliance, we transmute energetically as the sacredness of the design shifts our whole perspective of consciousness. Within one sacred moment of alliance to our Overlay, we go through a full transference of light consciousness. We get to take one more step within the many parallel universes that hold our full place of Home.

The expanded WE energy creates a further bonding energy with our Overlays. As we bring in our frequency of the WE energy we can reach through into the completed dimensional setting that the Overlay is anchored through. Remember our work with the energy of the WE in the second chapter. This energy activates our extended God element held within aspects of our Overlays. The WE holds the golden form of Truth. As we activate this multidimensional frequency by using the sound WE..., there is a profound expansion as we connect on a more complete level.

Then we can carry that full initiation energy through our heart. Our heart, Home Space, is known as the divine conductor to our multidimensional higher source Self. The pure frequency that is held within our new Blueprint supports our re-emergence through the blending process with our Overlay. It works in conjunction with our divine conductor, the Home Space, creating this new element of pure synergy of light flowing through us.

The access for us to align is the "space beyond reason" that allows us to anchor these individual roots from our Overlays. We anchor to this space using the three Conscious Breaths that automatically align us to our divine connector with our heart structure, our Home Space. The structure within this space can be likened to an open-ended cave, which is linked, woven energetically to our heart. Through our divine conductor within the heart we can move within this space, which moves us beyond our original earthly anchored aspect. We can align to the frequency held within the blue, golden light that is interwoven within the multidimensional aspect of the heart, linking us through to this space. Within this space we can enter an expansive consciousness that is held within a flow, which gives us deeper access into the Timeline realm, and entry into the moment where all things exist simultaneously.

Using our three Conscious Breaths we can become a deeper extension of the flow, opening us further into the powerful arena of the Timeline space. Remember that we can utilize the sound of WE and open up a deep and dynamic alliance process with an aspect of our Overlay design.

As we consciously choose to open into this action of alliance with one of our individual Overlays, the creation design bonds within us. Each Overlay holds a series of intricate patterns of creation that hold our completion energies. They are unique to our Higher Self. Each Overlay

carries individual aspects of our sacred makeup, and every Overlay structure carries awakening Truths that align us to a more expansive vision.
The Overlay holds the multidimensional form of Self. Now is the time for
us to begin a conscious choice journey realigning to these Overlays that
exist in other parallel Universes. Know that each parallel existence holds
essential connections for us to regain our full knowledge and power.

As we breathe into the Overlay design that is interconnected within our heart structure, the three Conscious Breaths will give us access
into the further unlimited space where all the collective design aspects
of creation can join with us. There is a doorway that will open within
the Overlay, and we enter using the sound WE…. We get to meet an expanded aspect of this paralleled expression within the experience. This is
a natural happening. The three Conscious Breaths will continue to adjust
us into position, and we are then able to line up through the different
Timeline within that paralleled existence.

This process can be likened to entering a twig of a tree. We are opening into a network of branches on the tree. This network gives you access into your multidimensional purpose design that is being utilized and
initiated through us simultaneously. At the same time, as we enter the
network we are automatically part of the full tree, the leaves, the trunk,
and all of the roots within the Earth. We absorb the full knowledge held
within the tree. We then become aware of the forest surrounding us and
know we are part of every aspect of that forest.

We will carry the multidimensional components and the geographical components of our parallel existence to each individual aspect of our
Overlay Self. Within the woven blue, golden frequency structure held
within our heart, all of these contacts to our Overlays are accessible within the doorway of our multidimensional heart container. Each time we
open into an Overlay there is a further extension birthed within the container of our heart.

This whole reawakening process is overseen through our Higher Self
principle that exists fully within the God Seat of Power. These components are pinpointed within our blue, golden frequency settings, which
are anchored within the aura of our heart. There is an invisible thread
connecting each aspect of our Higher Self within our individual Overlays.
Each aspect is lined up perfectly within the parallel existence settings

held within each Overlay form. Through our Timeline we will complete ourselves.

This information is essential right now for our evolution, to enable us to begin to consciously operate and exist within the full framework of our multidimensional nature, to anchor into the "space beyond reason" reconnecting to where we fully belong.

There are no time restraints that exist within the Collective Universes. Within our heart center structure is our full connection link to all aspects of our multidimensional selves that exist. Through our heart center we are naturally aligned to all aspects of Self, and can utilize the expression of the sacred that we are. There is no split that exists within us, because through all time continuums lies the Oneness State of Being. We are now being asked to embrace this aspect of our multidimensionality within the parallel Universes, to begin a witnessing of our different states of being that exist through our Overlays. This is time for us to begin the path of recollection, and enter this new realm of reconnection to full Truth of Self.

There is no time. There is a rhythm that breathes and flows, creating a Universal Time System where every experience exists within "the moment." Everything is woven within this rhythm, throughout one Timeless Master Overlay pattern. Within the Truth there is only one existence, held within the one Master Overlay pattern. You are, we are, there is but one movement between all the Collective Universes. We exist as the One, a Master Overlay pattern, which in Truth has never altered. Through this one Master Overlay pattern, we are held. We have always been held. All life force within the Collective Universes has been held through this Master Overlay. The God Seat of Power has woven itself through the pattern and has formed an encompassing love that creates a sacred seal within all.

This Truth is essential for us to comprehend, as it extends the invitation for a sacred union to evolve between each one of us on planet Earth. Every human being is interconnected within that one full Master Overlay design. There is to be an impeccability of action for all humanity, and this is to be exemplified by those of us who are awake.

Awakening means consciousness in action. For every conscious action there is a love reaction. We are all aware of this Truth. Now the reaction is one hundred fold as we begin to consciously align to our own personal Overlay designs. Our sacred power grows as we deepen and strengthen through our initiations with our Overlay designs. These redesigns that are birthing and reconfiguring our consciousness are an essential ingredient to returning consciously to the Master Overlay design. The Master Overlay design has always been in place; nothing changes the sacred format held within this pure, potent creation element.

A Simple Process in This Moment

1. Utilize the three Conscious Breaths right now and simply let go. You will feel a strong reaction within you of being lined up to this Truth of your parallel existence in the form of your sacred Overlays. Feel how the three Conscious Breaths create the experience of a doorway opening to your heart. You will begin to glimpse, sense, or see the energy of that light waiting for you. You will begin to perceive another aspect of this light of your self that has been hidden within the folds of the other world realities.

2. Begin to use the sound WE... just once into the space where you find yourself. Witness a further lining up within you, maybe a deepening of experience as you begin to align to the Timeline.

3. Bring the three Conscious Breaths into that space. Feel how this simple action of your breath allows you to claim the moment that has always existed when you choose to breathe in this way. This allows you to align to the Timeline deeply.

4. Open consciously to work within the WE energy by bringing in the sound WE.... In reality the WE energy is the interconnected link that brings you into that multidimensional parallel setting within the Timeline. Just be with this energy and feel yourself consciously being, as you open up to your Overlay.

Your own self-acceptance within the three Conscious Breaths is a paramount step to moving within the order of the One. This is Truth. WE are and you are the existence of the One.

Nothing exists outside of the reality of the One, only the One. You re-enter this state through the acceptance of what you have created for yourself. There is, in Truth, nothing more. You need to see what is right in front of you. There is the existence of simply the One within the moment. WE is the collective One, the purest form of Being.

Beyond the One we are. Beyond the Truth we are. Beyond existence we are. There is no time as we move beyond the Timeline to the limitless state of existence. WE are, WE move, WE belong to all that exists. WE claim what is there for all of us as the One. WE are, WE are the One.

The door is wide open for us. Changing our concept of where and how we exist within the Collective is paramount to being in the now, in the moment.

This is a new road for us to embark, opening our consciousness into our multidimensional existence, embracing our true heritage. Through embracing our paralleled existence we can reposition ourselves to the unlimited vision of connection to Truth. There is no other existence that is held within the purity of the God that we are. The return to a simple state of being is what is required of us to enter a sacred union of Truth.

WE... are the One. God is. WE... are. We claim that which is holy within us through the realignment to our own paralleled existence within our own multidimensional state.

Note: You   can   find   an   audio   file   link   at *www.christinedayonline.com/pleiadianpromise* Listen to the audio file for this chapter. The audio file contains a multidimensional quality that will allow you to work through the different levels of initiations with your Overlays. Each time you work with this audio you will expand, further initiating into more Overlays within your Timeline.

Chapter 11

The Unveiling

Through our reconnection to the series of sacred Overlays we have undergone a reconstruction of our energetic centers. Each one of us is now able to move forward onto new pathways of our destiny. This reconnection to our place within the Collection Universes has been partially realized, which has released us permanently from the anchored illusion that has kept us in a state of separation on Earth. This liberation has brought us into an ability to transmit this energy of Truth outward to humanity.

The illusion of life that we have lived up to this point can now be part of our past experience. This is our time to embrace the changes that have taken place within us. We can begin creating a shift on the planet through our own personal transformation, opening a new flow around us that brings in the New Dawning energy to be anchored and self-realized in our outer world. Our planet Earth is ready for great change and a strong element of that change must first come from within us. We are able to re-enter the Collective Universal Community with our realignment to that understanding of Truth. We have become an extension of that Truth.

We are able to embrace the fullness of carrying these sacred alignments of our place within the Collective Universes on a deeper level within our cells. As we hold the essence of Truth we begin to anchor and move this energy consciously throughout the planet.

We began to regain our power, our insight, in a more complete form through the initiations from our individual Overlays. We have become interwoven into that Collective design, which enables us to begin to source from that which is the sacred weave, and extends throughout the Universes. We can draw from the sacred imprint that is part of our signature, which makes up part of this weave. Utilizing this imprint is an essential requirement for our planetary work.

Our individual transformation strongly impacts the planet in the larger scheme of things. We each play a powerful role on the planet because of our evolution, and it is essential that we individually, consciously witness and acknowledge ourselves in our self-realization process. Like a rising sun, our rays go outward, gently touching humanity, impacting the dense areas on the earth plane, shifting the dimensional energies through the geographical areas throughout our world.

We as the "way showers" have become the light. We are bringing the sacred connection from the Collective Universes to the planet through our frequency signature light generated by the Truth that we are now a part. Each one of us is to bring our signature light, birthed through our Overlays, onto the planet. We have always been destined to play a pivotal role in our own resurrection of the Earth. This is a sacred action, the forging of the light in this New Dawning era.

We carry the understanding of the full role illusion has had on this Earth. We hold the energy of Truth within and we hold the Platform, like a mirror, for dramatic change to take place with all humanity. The illusion has been strongly played out with the elements of separation and limitation preventing us from believing in the vastness of Self. Now this light of Truth has permeated through our very hearts, moving outward and emanating like the rays of the Sun.

The ego mind may want to discourage us from being certain of our role as a catalyst for change; however, this is our perfectly divine orchestrated timing to begin consciously anchoring this aspect of the New Dawning.

We as human beings have always needed to be the ones to hold and convey this Truth to each other. This was always going to be our role, transmitting Truth. This was always the plan: to activate and bring forth our own self-resurrection within our Community here on Earth.

Now is the time for new Communities to form; we carry the mirrored imprint within our hearts for the forming of these new Communities. Through our transformed consciousness we will hold a space for humanity to open up and participate within these Community bases.

There are many forms of sacred Communities that make up the full network within the Collective Universes. There has been a holy design forged within all those Communities, which is dominated and overseen by the central force of the God Seat of Power. This Community design is, in reality, not separate from us. We have been in separation from this design. In Truth, we have always been part of this extended Community within the Collective Universes. They have been holding this sacred pact with us, with the commitment to support us in our unfolding journey of forming our own sacred Community design.

This process is a collective mission that is essential for all of us within the Collective Universes. We play an integral role as part of this full Community. The plan has always been in place for the forming of new conscious Communities on Earth that will mirror the sacred energy design within the Communities of the Collective Universes.

Each one of us who are the "way showers" has a key role to play in the successful forming of sacred Communities here on our planet. Some of us have the role of carrying this transmitting component of the sacred design of Community within our hearts, holding this mirror of Community design steady for humanity. Others will actively engage in creating and overseeing the Community development design. Some will support the anchoring of energies for the individual Communities to be created. The God Seat of Power holds in place the sacred energetic design for Communities on Earth. We each hold a living aspect of the God Seat within the structure of our heart Home Space, for the very purpose of the creation of these new Communities.

Through stabilizing and expanding our interactions within the Universes we will build and gain a stronger inner-core connection to our unique place within the entire Collective Communion energy. We will be able to deepen our sense of belonging to this Universal Community as we begin to glimpse ourselves in a new way, by opening up a doorway to a more profound aspect of our signature Self.

The forming of individual Communities here on the earth plane is dependent on us first building and refining our alignments with the Universal Communities. Through our evolution of relationships within the Collective Universes we will get to directly experience our extended Community of Home. As we unfold we will carry the frequency of Community alive within our hearts, like a reflecting mirror. As we foster our relationships with the individual life force groups within the Universal Communities, we will learn and unfold through these experiences. We can then bring the same energetic dynamics that are held within their Communities to create our own Community design.

We all hold this energetic design within us for the new base for Community development on our planet. This design will assist us in gaining healthy, productive connections for our relationship building of Communities here. We will also be able to bring a refined energetic communion connection through our direct experience from the Universal Communities.

Eventually there will be no separation between us and the rest of the multiple Communities that exist within the Collective Universes. As we evolve here on planet Earth, we will actively engage, working with other life force group Communities. This happening has been pre-ordained through the sacred texts held within the God Seat of Power.

We on planet Earth have this energetic Truth imprinted through the structure within our hearts. This energetic imprint will begin to mirror this Truth outward at a certain juncture within the framework of this New Dawning era, enabling us to meet our destiny and return to take our full place within the Collective Universes.

Up to this point our planet has played out the illusion of separation fully. We have seen ourselves made up as a series of completely individual communities divided by the barriers of land and oceans. Within our countries we have separated ourselves within these communities by creating provinces, villages, and neighborhoods where we have further separated out in the name of religion, race, color, and socioeconomic status.

All of humanity is being held by the sacred consciousness of the God Seat of Power located within the central Universes. We are being bathed by this reflected light, which transfers the energy of Truth, which is a natural state of union for humanity to align. Those who are awakened carry this active imprint design within us, enabling us to take this huge step forward collectively to reach our goal.

By working with our Overlays we automatically begin to respond energetically to the imprint that we carry. The Imprint aligns us to the Collective Community design. Naturally we will begin to move into the pivotal role that we are to play through our Imprint. We are opened into our sacred connection to the God Seat of Power as we consciously move into reunion with the Collective Universal Communities, witnessing our partnership. This is the beginning of our true Homecoming within the Collective Universes.

This Homecoming process opens the way for us to then reconnect to humanity as a whole. We are exposed to a Truth that contains the unrelenting pure force of the Oneness, Collective God Consciousness that is interwoven within each human form on our planet. We get to witness in action the innate pulse that extends through each one of us. In reality, we are this aspect of the One.

The Pleiadians have set out an energetic format for us to follow, and they have given us a series of step-by-step directives for the successful anchoring of these new Communities to be established. This process will support the birthing and development of these new Communities that are destined to grace our earth plane in this New Dawning era. A Truth is we each hold within us the potential for the development of energetic Core bases that are to carry the designs for our new Communities here on Earth.

Some of these new energetic structures are already birthing and have anchored within the cells of our physical body to support us in this mission. These energetic designs have begun to move this frequency onto the planet to support the changes that will be taking place as we begin this awakening. These designs are aligning through the consciousness of those who will be actively involved, who will play a significant role in forming these Community bases.

These frequencies held within the designs provide a container that will enable those of us who are ready to form Core Groups. Each Core Group's mission is to activate an energetic Platform to manifest an anchor for the unfolding of a series of new Community structures. These Platforms will act as transmitters, channeling the sacred communion design from the Universes, which will activate the New Dawning consciousness within individual Community settings. The process of these Platforms has been set in place to reestablish this holy form of communion through our new Communities on planet Earth.

The Platform works within the heart, Home Space structure of each individual that holds an active Imprint, containing an aspect of the God Seat of Power. The Platform plays the essential role of transferring these pure frequencies of consciousness that exist for all Communities within the Universes. This reawakens that which has been lying dormant within us here on Earth. The Platform will anchor the sacred scripts within our new Communities slowly, gradually transferring those pure frequencies of love throughout the Community, as they are being absorbed within the planet.

This love reveals a series of pathways for an unfolding communion to be self-realized within individuals who are ready to reopen their telepathic centers. All communication within the Collective Universes happens through their telepathic communion centers. We are to reestablish our natural abilities for telepathic communion within our own Communities. The telepathic communion holds the highest and purest frequencies of love, which carries only Truth. Our natural Blueprints sustain that full capacity, that love component that is held within communion. We will naturally realign back into that which is sacred within our communication with each other.

Each Community will have its own individual Platform that contains a preordained timing that has been set in place for their unique Community network. This timing has been established for their personal Community awakening, lifting the veils of illusion further as each individual Community is ready to anchor and then transform.

There is a sacred realignment that is destined to be forged between the Collective Universes and us. Through the raising of our frequency to the framework of this collective energy our Communities can connect, and return us to our full place within the Universes for our completion.

We belong. We have always been a part of this expanded multidimensional Community that is within the Collective Universes. With the development of new Communities on Earth we will be able to directly experience our place, our unique resonance to the sacred frequencies contained within the full design held through this conscious communion within the Universes.

The Pleiadians hold in place this format for the sacred design of Earth. They are holding the energy of this design to ensure the complete transition of our Community bases here on the planet, for us to fully re-establish our sacred heritage Origin connections.

The Spiritual Realms will play many roles. They are able to work with us through the openings created within the individual Platforms that will be held within each Community group. The Christ resurrection energy will play a significant role in our unfolding process, bringing us through a doorway to another aspect of Self. Mother Mary brings a higher frequency of love through the Platform, expanding our heart centers dimensionally, in order to accelerate our Community communion connections with each other. Other Spiritual Realm energies, Angels, Light Beings, and Masters are also able to access us through the Platforms and work in alliance with individuals within our Community settings.

The natural elements of the Sun, Earth, wind, fire, and water all carry strong essences for the accelerated unfolding to support our integration process within this transitional phase. The plants, trees, and rocks all hold energetic settings to support the development of these new Community bases. They are specifically designed to assist those of us that are going through this rapid awakening through the reconnection to our Overlays. These supportive energies will enable the individual Community groups to form and come together, allowing each one to play their full role within a Core group setting. They hold an energetic arena for the creation and anchoring of the many Platforms for the new Communities to form.

This is a dynamic format being sustained by the Pleiadians, allowing these designs to successfully create an evolution for us and allowing humanity to begin to thrive within these new Communities. There is to be no hierarchy within these Community designs. Each person will be seen as equal and will carry their unique divine signature frequency, each contributing to society on an energetic level.

There will, of course, be a disparity between the unfolding of the individual enlightenment levels: with some that have already attained a level of self-mastery, and in others the unfulfilled potential yet to be self-realized. Regardless of where a person is within his or her own enlightenment process, each person makes up a vital part of the Community energy. Everyone naturally and equally contributes their individual sacred divine signature, which holds the unique element that will always be a contributing factor to each Community. Our signature elements are held within the multidimensional heart structure so every one of us carries our full frequency signature, regardless of where we are in our enlightenment path.

Through the structured Community Platform, we will be automatically aligned to that collective energy, which is connected to the element of the God Seat of Power. There is an element of that connection that exists within our heart, Home Space structure, and because of this, we will automatically transmit our frequency signature, contributing to our Community. This is a natural process that is activated from our Higher Self and is supported through the framework that is mirrored from the Community Platform.

The initial activation of the Platform process is continually stabilized and held by the Core group members of each Community. There will be an ongoing unfolding, an evolutionary process that takes place within each Community member through the Platform. The pure energy that is radiated out from the Platform deepens and expands the communion experience, which allows the Community to flourish.

The dimensional setting on the planet will change as the individual Communities develop and mature. This will create a series of "lifting of veils," which will move the entire Community into a higher dimensional environment. Like a curtain going up on a stage, there will be revelations of Truth opening up for all within that Community.

As these veils collectively lift, the illusion of density will be released from the environment of Earth. Those who have not previously been awake will suddenly "awaken from the dream." The dream has been living this third-dimensional illusionary life. They will awaken from the dream and remember who they are from that higher perspective of Truth. They will simply slip back into that higher reality of themselves. This will be a natural awakening.

We are the sacred happening. We carry the gifts of this time that is woven within our heart structures. Nothing can stand in the way of this successful evolution. The timing is perfect and the call goes outward to all of you on your path to come and play with this next phase of your mission.

As our new Communities are developed through the individual Platforms, we will begin to hold a steady alignment to Truth that has always existed within the holy consciousness of the Collective Universes. The plan is for humans to consciously reestablish our connections to Home, which lies at the very center of the Collective Universes, held within the God Seat of Power.

Our new Communities will operate from a new perspective, from a deep innate knowing that will be mirrored through the Community Platform. This Platform will interact directly within the structures held through the hearts of humanity. We each hold the Imprint design for the sacred that we are, within our hearts.

Many of us hold the sacred timing for participating in this mission of becoming a part of a Core group to create Platforms for Communities. We will feel a new level of fulfillment because our individual heart's desire will be activated by us by playing this role. We will be fulfilled as we experience the deep Truth of our God Consciousness state as it becomes self-realized. Through being part of the Core group we will get to witness our selves and the unending strength that exists within. We will get to experience the unlimited aspect of our sacred, as the energy forms and moves within each individual as they align to the Platform we are holding. We will go through a reconfiguration, a metamorphic unfolding of Self, as we begin to line up to the full multidimensional mirroring that is held by our Community Platform.

Each Core group will continue to evolve as it holds the Platform for its Community. Our deep, inner desire to return to what we originally have always been will propel each one of us forward more completely into this transforming role.

The plan is that every Community Platform will form a synergetic alliance with each other. Each Platform will resonate a pulse and will naturally interact through a common synergy of light. This birth will form an enormous giant golden web that opens up a fluid womb around the Earth. We will be held and embraced through this interconnected webbing, immersed by the holy energies of the One. As this full womb expresses itself, humanity will be enabled to return to its fully transmuted state of consciousness. This will recalibrate our vibration back to Home base within the Collective Universes.

The Pleiadians call us the "way showers." Through re-entering our sacred divine connections that are held within the Collective Universes we will forge our way homeward, anchoring through our place of origin. This is an essential happening that will enable us, as members of the Core group, to hold an optimum space of consciousness for the mirroring to take place with our original Communities.

An aspect of the extension of planned Communities is for us to awaken to our place within the extended Community within the Collective Universes. This invitation extends to all of us as a human group. We take our place consciously as a collective "life force group" and begin to open into our full neighborhood setting within the Universes.

We will continue to have our human journey; however, we will be moving into a new phase of existence with our human element. There will be a natural evolution with the human aspect forming a relationship with the sacred that we have always been. As we are consciously awakened, we will hold our human aspect with a true love and compassion, changing the inner dynamic within us. Ending the internal wars and separation enables us to reconnect to Home. We are to honor the full sacredness of our journey.

Community Pattern Activation

Note: There can be a maximum of twenty-four people to be part of your Core group to hold the Platform for your Community Pattern to be activated. There can be a minimum number of three people for your Core group.

What Is Holding the Platform?

Those of you who have worked and initiated with your Overlays carry the frequency initiations from the "space beyond reason." You hold the Imprint design energy anchored by the God Seat of Power within. This energy is housed within the structure of your heart, Home Space, and acts as a mirror, reflecting and holding the full energy of the Platform for Community.

This process of holding your Imprint design energy enables you to activate the Community Pattern energy, playing your role by being part of the Core group. You hold the Platform for the whole Community. As you facilitate the activation with your Core group, you move into the role of naturally holding the energy of the Platform stable between you as a Core group. This energy moves through your own heart, Home Space structure and transmits the Imprint design through the Platform, anchoring the energetic design of the God Seat of Power for the entire Community.

This is holding the Platform, which is a natural process that does not draw any energy from you personally. Rather, this links directly to your Higher Self energy sourcing through the Imprint design held within your heart, Home Space. This directly transmits through the Platform and opens up into the individual community members. Working with the Community Pattern further activates and expands this transmission of the universal design for Community.

Birthing of Your Core Group

Note: There are six positions on the Community Pattern, labeled A through F (see the diagram on page 180). If there are only the minimum of three people as the Core group, they position themselves on A, C, E. This positioning forms a natural triangle between the three people.

Each person stands aligned to his or her position (for example: A, C, E). Each person stands the same distance away from their position, so the triangular form is balanced between the three of them. If there are four or five people making up the Core group, then those people come into B, D, or F positions. If there are any unfilled positions, the Pleiadians will come in to take those empty positions for the forming of your Core group energy. If there are six or more people, you first fill the six positions, A through F. Then the extra person or additional people stand directly behind the others in their positions. They stand directly behind the person that is lined up to any one of the positions, A through F.

Note: The Pleiadians will fill any open, remaining positions. For example, if you have 24 people (this is the maximum you can have to be part of the Core group to activate and hold the Platform), you will have four people lined up to each position, from A through F.

This process is done between those of you who are in the first place at the six positions marked A through F.

1. You will all bring your awareness into the Central Pattern. Use your Conscious Breath and place it within the Central Pattern, then let go. Keep letting go within the Central Pattern.

2. You will all bring the sacred sound, AE TEASH, into the Central Pattern. Feel the birthing of this energy activate through you. Feel the Core energy begin to birth between all of you that are in the first positions, A through F. Keep using the sacred sound until the Core energy between you feels complete; that means the energy is no longer building between you.

3. Then if you have other people behind you as part of your Core group, you move out of your position to stand at the end of your same line. They move forward to stand in the front position and you repeat the process with those people now activating through the Central Pattern with the sacred sound. When the Core energy has completed on yet another level that group of six people moves to the back of the line. The next group moves forward into position and opens into the activation of the Central Pattern with the sacred sound. Your Core group will build and expand with each of the activations with all Core group members participating. There is a strong letting-go energy required as the full Core group is anchored for your Community.

Final Process for Forming Core Group

All Core group members bring their awareness once more into the Central Pattern. Feel a connecting link within the Core group and now everyone is to use the sound AE TEASH. Use the sound as many times as needed until the Core energy is fully anchored through each of you.

Note: If you have six or fewer Core group members you will only do one round of activating your Core group. If you have seven to twelve Core group members you will do two rounds to activate your full Core group. If you have thirteen to eighteen Core group members you will do three rounds to activate your full Core group. If you have nineteen to twenty-four Core group members you will do four rounds.

Activation of Your Community Pattern

All Core group members stand surrounding the Community Pattern design circle. In the same placement that you activated your Core group. You are now going to activate your Community Platform by listening to the audio file link. Each one of the Core group members needs to let go during this process.

Note: You can find an audio file link at *www.christinedayonline.com/pleiadianpromise* Use this audio file to work with your Core Group to birth your Platform. You only need to utilize with the audio file one time. However, you will need to work with the audio file again if you have a new Core group member join to hold your Platform for your Community.

Community Pattern Design

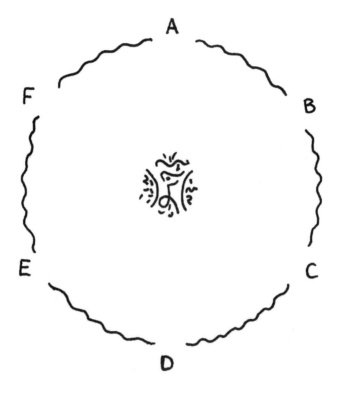

Sound: AE TEASH

Chapter 12

Unearthed

We originally were birthed through a sacred flow that existed beyond the Collective Universes, and we were breathed into existence. We were moved, positioned to our original design within the Collective Universes. We were then bathed within a current of pure life force. We were cradled within the Central Universes by the God Seat of Power while being initiated into the full form of our unique sacred consciousness. We were blessed, kissed by the light, being made manifest, as we became the light. We were embraced by our life force group family, and received in love.

Now is the time for us to rejoin this flow and align back into the moment of our original conception, to return and consciously experience being held within our unique current of light, being moved back to the sacred multidimensional frequency of our true Origin. This is our time to re-emerge through the unlimited Timeless space that is our Home.

Our unique frequency current, which carries the sacred flow of our individual design, is programmed to move us through a series of pathway initiations. This enables us to awaken and begin to source our own signature container of Self. There is an intense, deep yearning within our heart, Home Space structure that has been activated, compelling us, calling us to return to our original roots.

We will be drawn by this distinct current through the openings of many dimensional doorways of light, consciously arriving to our Homecoming. Our original roots are held in the form of a pure, expansive, fluid signature consciousness, which is interwoven within the Collective Universes and held by the God Seat of Power. This aspect of our Origin self holds the complete form of our sacred. We will be reconstructed through a series of multidimensional layers of consciousness.

Within our human experience there have often been feelings of being unfulfilled. There has been a part of us that has been searching, questioning, and reaching out within our experiences to discover if there is something more. This state of unrest is, in Truth, a deep inner calling for a reconnection to our true origin—a call for us to return to our spiritual heritage roots where we originated, and to align once more to the aspect of Self that has always existed. We are ready to finally reconnect to our state of wholeness.

There has been a great resistance within our human element to let go and change, to become part of that greater aspect of Self. Now we are being given the revelation to open to Truth, that our true origin is not from Earth. We need to embrace this repositioning and reorientation of our consciousness and begin to open to this reconnection, which is our true heritage origin. To consciously return to a place where we were originally seeded beyond this planet.

Yes, we have come to this planet to have a human experience. However, we can no longer operate from the limited mindset associated with being human. It is time to let go of this incorrect belief that our connection to humanity equates to where we original were rooted. There is not one human being on this planet that originated from Earth. A Truth is, we all have our origins with other life force groups within the Collective Universes.

This limited thought process, that we originated from Earth, has restricted us in our evolution. This belief has prevented us from aligning to our sacred aspect that has always authentically existed within the Collective Universes. Through this misperception we have stopped ourselves from participating within our true worlds where our full authentic Self resides.

We can no longer use the measure of what is normal by Earth's standards because this reality is steeped in illusion. This revelation launches us into an authentic collective framework. This allows us to be freed to unearth ourselves, so that we get to experience a completely new energetic movement of conscious connection with our true heritage origin. The energy of this Truth will expand and open another space within our heart structure. This space will lead us to our reconnection to the birthed current that will align us back to our roots.

There is a profound sacred movement that will open within our hearts as we embrace this undeniable new thought process of our true origin. As our hearts begin to be enlivened by this Truth a new energetic pulse is birthed, which holds that design of our sacred roots.

Within the heart is a container in a form of the Holy Chalice. As we unearth ourselves and allow this Truth to unfold within our consciousness, our multidimensional sacred design within the Chalice begins to light up in response. Within this Chalice is a pure consciousness that carries the true frequency of our origin settings. These settings have been lying dormant, actively waiting for us to open and come into this self-realized moment.

We are ready to move into a next phase of our spiritual maturity, to claim our true state of origin. As we access these energetic activations and open to what is contained within our Chalice, there is an authentic dimensional setting that we will automatically begin tapping into. This aligns us to our true expanded power center, which has been holding the coordinates to where we were seeded within our true origin heritage settings.

Through the Chalice we will be guided back to our original roots, to an essential aspect of our being that is found within our life force group family. We were originally sourced through the Collective Communion of the One. When we unearth ourselves, we will be liberated, and no longer weighed down by the illusion that we originated from Earth. We will be returned to the One.

Within this state of Truth, we will begin to encounter another viewpoint of Self. There will be a repositioning and reorientation of our senses, as we are moved laterally into an altered and pure experience of this more expansive, fuller design of Self. There will be the need for adjustments within ourselves as we align back to this profoundly different state of being. We will be entering an environment that will require us to deeply let go of all that we have known consciously in our limited illusionary experiences thus far. We will, however, get to witness and move into a self-discovery as we remerge into our origin life force group family.

Each one of these life force family groups lives beyond the third-dimensional illusion, and they interact through telepathic communion. Each individual within their communities carries a specific divine frequency that contributes to the Community. Every individual is seen as an equal, and is honored for the unique qualities that they carry. Each member contributes differently but there is a commonality of the One, held between each person. This element creates a natural union between all. Through their innate telepathic communion abilities there is a common flow and purpose. There is a sacred pact, an alignment between the full group energy.

Our individual place within our Family of Light is being anchored open through our Higher Self. Our conscious return to our origin family will strongly impact the entire Community energy. As we return to our family origin it is important to know that we will continue to exist within our human framework on Earth. As we become conscious of living out a simultaneous existence within our family of origin, we still have an essential part to play on this planet.

Truth is, there is no separation. We are all part of the One. Within this Truth, we will bring to humanity the vibration of love that will be alive within us from our reconnection to Home. We will resurrect our relationship first through our own human element, and then transfer this outwards to other humans.

This conscious alignment to the Chalice within our heart structure will act as an energetic compass navigating us back through to our own unique multidimensional Timeline, returning us to our origin. We get to return to our original Community through the Timeline, to our Family of Light, which is where we have always existed in our completed form.

The plan has always been to reconnect to our origin. As we go through a reorientation to our Family of Light group, we will begin an assimilation and expansion process as we re-experience our original pure consciousness connection. We can expect a deep inner transformation as we engage with these higher frequencies of connection through the new perceptions of our telepathic communion to our origin group. We will be able to engage with our authentic, holy origin that exists within the full Community Universes. This will be a completely natural re-bonding experience with our family of origin, bringing us into a profound reopening to forms of Self.

We have never been separated from our origin, but we have been disconnected from the direct experience of Being. We will move into the rediscovery of our roots, with our life force group family within this Collective. As we consciously own the Truth of our heritage and are received through our Homecoming to our original Family of Light, we will move into a more complete expression of Self.

Hundreds of thousands of life force groups exist that make up the full contingency of the Collective Universes. All of these life force groups are interconnected to each other through the God Seat of Power. They each carry a unique aspect of the force of the One within them. As we return to our true family of origin, there is an energetic evolution flowing within the entire Community of the One, and we become more whole within ourselves. There will be a revolutionary action by the divine element anchoring, shifting the multidimensional proportions within the entire Collective Community. This divine element will weave itself and interact throughout all life force.

This return by us creates a seal of completion within the framework of our family of origin. Each one of us will be this essential, unique component within our Community. As we re-enter, we complete the whole within the Community. As a completed Community we can transition further dimensionally within the deeper folds of the God Seat of Power. We will all take a next step forward within our Community of origin, transforming within the divine-content as we are self-realized through this return to family.

There are many other individuals who are presently residing on Earth who are from the same Origin family, within the same life force group, as we are. As we encounter those individuals from the same origin family group, we will experience a strong, powerful, magnetic draw—a heartfelt connection between them and us. Many pre-agreements have been made between those of us from the same origin family who are coming together at this time. We will enable each other to open deeply within our hearts and hold a unique form of love that exists within our Family of Light from Home. We will come together to form alliances and activate these pre-agreements. We will be able to energetically work together, forming a strong, natural synergy of resonance because we are from the same origin family. This will enable us to forge a stronger anchor of light between us and hold a Platform for a pathway to open up for others to also realign to their family of origin.

There will be many individuals gathering from the same life force group, naturally drawn together by the recognition of similar signature energies. These signatures are held within the Chalice through their heart structure. As they form alliances through this common energetic bond, they are able to forge a mirrored communion. Through this mirror they create a beacon of light for others who also belong to this same life force group to be drawn. This forming of the mirrored energy acts like a compass, transmitting light.

Some Core groups will be made up of one specific life force family group. An aspect of some pre-agreements within groups is to create Platforms to form specific new Communities on Earth. These specific Communities will be designed to mirror out to other Communities the power of this sacred union, and act as a role model for others to follow. These designed Core groups will also play a unique role by enabling individuals to align to their pathways in order to reconnect to their origin roots, to their family life force groups. Together the Core group will hold the collective force of energy to launch and anchor others through this Platform design to their origin of Home.

Our individual origin life force family group is aware of our existence here on the planet. They are actively supporting us as family members of light. They await our conscious return, knowing the sacred place that we occupy within our Community is playing an essential role for all.

Through these specific pre-agreements with our own life force group family, a pact was formed and we are brought back into an expanded reality alignment to the Sacred. We planted ourselves like a seed in the soil within our origin. We originated from that seed in our Home base with our Family of Light. This action, held within this pact, is what enables us now to return, opening consciously into this enlightened aspect of Self through our family of origin.

This Self exists in paralleled Universes. As we consciously recognize and acknowledge the existence of our true origins we are revealed through the full self-realization of our roots. Through this opening is the natural action of aligning to all multidimensional forms of Self. This can be likened to the full blossoming of the flower, the petals opening fully, extending itself to the Sun.

Through this recognition of our multidimensional form we can operate within these physical bodies on the planet. However, we will go through a complete energetic and physical metamorphosis as this process is unfolding and as we are being unveiled to our selves. We will naturally be able to carry the expanded expression of our fully awakened Self now. This process will completely free us, unearthing us from the illusion on Earth.

This current time frame in our evolution requires a focused intention on our own self-discovery as we move forward and mature. There is a revolutionary change in our relationship with the Collective Universes as we consciously evolve into our original roots. As we open consciously to our roots through the Chalice within the Timeline, we can begin the active process of unearthing ourselves. As we reach outward with our consciousness through the Time Line we begin this new phase of our journey. As we align to our Chalice we open up into navigating toward our family of origin, to Home.

Through our direct experience of "knowing" that our origins are not from Earth and they never have been, we will move forward. We will open on a liberated pathway, as we are no longer held in the restriction of illusion regarding our roots. We will move on an avenue of rediscovering Self and embracing that, which ultimately forms our Holiness.

There is a deepening process for us to unravel within, to explore who we are within our multidimensional selves within our family of origin. We will find these answers through our roots. We will be ready to access these revelations through this new perspective of Truth. As we dispel all aspects of separation from the Collective we will allow another level of expression of our creativity, through the engagement within our roots. We will reach our goal of coming Home to Self.

There is a need to explore and then integrate what this Truth means to us on a human level. What does this bring to us within the reality of our current life on Earth?

My Experience

As I unveiled my own origin, and re-aligned to my expanded life force group of my Family of Light, I entered a deep experience of the joyful expression of Self. Opening into my Pleiadian heritage and reconnecting to my family origin changed me forever, as I explored the powerful aspect of Self. I have been in a conscious and active communion with my Pleiadian Family of Light while simultaneously living out my human existence. I have been actively engaged in my mission, strongly supported by my natural gifts that have anchored through me from my Origin Self. I went through a complete transformation while anchoring my full Pleiadian self within my physical and energetic body.

As I opened up to the energies within this chapter, carrying this essential information of our individual origins, I was deeply moved inside my heart. This revelation was a surprise to me. I had not considered that all humans had their origins off planet Earth. I had assumed incorrectly that some humans had originated from Earth.

The energy of this Truth filled me with tremendous emotion. I opened into the enormity of what this understanding means to many of you and the impact, the difference it will make to your lives, and to your individual path of awakening. I could feel and appreciate the deep love that is contained within this Truth.

As I let go into the fullness of this revelation an amazing opening occurred within me. I was being bathed in this pure loving force. As I let go further into this profound element of love I found myself being propelled into a huge transformational arena. My Pleiadian family was surrounding me, and I found myself in a central chamber of light where I was being initiated into a fuller state of my Pleiadian Self. I was being acknowledged, lifted up, and anointed through the God Seat of Power and birthed into a new form of Self.

After this profound process I realized that I had set myself free on yet another level through my willingness to open to this new understanding about humanity. This Truth allowed me to somehow become more aligned to my own love, my own abundance within my Pleiadian Home. I was able to receive myself with awe and a great appreciation for my sacred connections to my origin home, to my Family of Light in a higher dimensional form.

Just know how much I honor this journey of self-discovery that we all are a part of. I send blessings and love to each one of you as you take your steps forward to Home.

The full veils are lifting for many of us, and this shifting of the energetic settings on the planet will enable us all to make these changes. We are ready for this new experience of understanding our original roots, embracing the energy of this Truth. We actually begin this new phase of our journey by first processing this information. Then we move our consciousness outward beyond our planet to engage with our origin family within our life force group. We need to embrace this aspect of our unique spirituality by directly experiencing how we belong and can thrive through our original life force group family. We will consciously begin to interact through communion with our family oforigin.

This communion process will create an opening of our awareness, of our natural state, our omnipresence. This is where we arise from the very center to Self and we will merge to our inner power. This inner part of Self arises and is central to the God Seat of Power within the Universes. Through this direct experience we will open to the feeling of belonging deeply within our heart. This is designed to bring us sustenance now, like receiving nutrition specifically for our heart. This will create within us a deeply satisfying settling within our Being. We have been yearning to come Home!

We need to experience our full spiritual life force within our origin group, where our true roots exist, within the Timeline held by the Collective Universes. The Time Line setting holds us within a fluid state of being, in which we function through our parallel existence, within this timeless, limitless space.

We have always existed as an aspect of the One God Consciousness element and in this supreme setting we flourish and continually expand through the God Seat of Power. Through returning consciously to our origin setting we will begin a lining up to all the multidimensional aspects of us that exists within all time settings. The parallel lives we are living, line up simultaneously through Self. The return to our original family will allow our sacred completion energy to finally merge together, bringing all elements of consciousness within us on a multidimensional level.

As all aspects of our multidimensionality merge, this alignment is the holy aspect of Self being self-realized. This is a historic happening for the completion of Self within our individual and collective evolutionary experience. These energetic changes strongly influence the unfolding of sacred formations shifting through the Collective Universes.

As we move through this evolutionary process an energetic form of Self will be held within the realms of the Collective Universes through our new alliance with the God Seat of Power. We will become an extended instrument within the Collective Imprint, as we access an untapped form of Self. We are the sum total of all elements that exist within the Universes. Our uniqueness flows, and is interwoven within the Timelines that are held and anchored in a continuous multidimensional line. We each exist as part of this weave and become more a part of the intricacies of this interwoven form as we continue to evolve.

This unveiling carries the energy of the Promise that the Pleiadians are imparting to us for our self-realized moment. This is the time for our own unveiling, remembering that within the moment all things exist in the unlimited Timeline. Through this Timeline all aspects of us can be rearranged simultaneously through our own conscious intention of knowing. We open to the moment and reform into this alliance with Self.

As we "unearth" ourselves we unravel into Truth. We will then be processed into an expanded state of receivership. We naturally align to our abundance through the fullness held within all aspects of Self. We receive that which is rightfully ours, opening like a flower to the sun to receive all that has been always been waiting for us. Now is our time to utilize that part of Self that is within the expanded existence of the moment.

We are continually being held within our own individual unfolding journeys. It is essential that we take full ownership of that which we have created, opening up to that which we have withheld from our selves until now, and celebrating the impeccability of our timing, for this revelation of Truth that is leading us back to our origin Self.

An essential aspect of this specific phase of the New Dawning is our full alignment back to our very central core roots of our origin. There is nothing more important right now. Our Homecoming is in front of us to achieve.

In order to move successfully forward and take this next step we must put our complete focus on letting go into the energy that is contained within the Chalice that exists in our heart structure, and to consciously reach out to our life force group. We may not have an active awareness of our family of origin; however, as we bring our conscious energy outward, our Chalice within our heart will begin to activate a guiding frequency aligning us back to our origin.

We need to be fully involved with the energetic aspect of our origin settings that are being transmitted through our Chalice. By simply letting go we will be linked naturally back within the guidance of the flow.

As we are received Home by our original Community, there will be a support system in place to recalibrate and re-orientate us to the full multidimensional Truth of who we are within our origin frequency setting. We will need to explore, through direct experience, how this new conscious connection will impact our current life setting.

As we engage in our process it is important that the drama of life on Earth doesn't sidetrack us. Rather, let go and allow a breaking away of old shells. There is a call going out to each one of us to leave everything behind on a third-dimensional level. Allow a "shedding of skins" that have been held in place through the varied limited misperceptions of our humanity. To let go and simply witness a falling away of illusion, like a cloak that has been wrapped around us, just dropping off.

As we let go and endeavor to express ourselves within the newness of our self-discovery we will bring to our life the energy of our roots of origin. As this origin-energy life force takes seed in our heart structure there will be a natural happening of self-transformation anchoring through our consciousness. We will find a clarity and peace that we have been waiting for through this alignment to the sacred that we are.

The more we let go, the more we can expand and anchor these new alignments through our cells, bringing a new awareness and freedom to our day-to-day lives. This release from density will enable our completion energy from our origin Self to anchor through our physicality. Through the reconnection to our origin state, this light frequency imprint will be anchored energetically through our systems.

We must continue to hold our human element while we unfold and allow space for new reconstruction of this form of Self. By the honoring of our humanity there will be a natural, redefined element birth within us. Our human aspect will evolve by experiencing an unfolding love through our sacred reconnection to our origin Self.

All of us within humanity have been supported through our collective experience. We will continue to play out this process of our awakening together to complete this New Dawning process of returning Home and anchoring our homecoming on Earth. Humanity holds the common element of the God Consciousness Communion, and through this Truth we all exist within different life force groups within the Universes.

Our time is here and now, to unearth our selves from any illusion that we are limited. We are internally, energetically prepared to achieve this now. The truth sets us free, propelling us into the realignment to our roots. We have all requested this illusion and we came to Earth to have the full experience of limitation. Now we get to witness ourselves becoming consciously "unearthed" and moving forward Home.

Note: You can find an audio file link at *www.christinedayonline.com/pleiadianpromise* The audio file will support you in the alignment to the Chalice that will navigate you back through the Timeline to your origin heritage. I will be guiding you, aligning you to your own Family of Light, within your life force group.

Know that you can listen to this audio file many times. The audio holds multidimensional frequencies that are designed to align you deeper and deeper to your origin-energy of Self within your Family of Light.

Blessings, and enjoy the journey!

APPENDIX:
ONGOING WORK WITH CHRISTINE

Numerous avenues are available for you to experience and to receive the ongoing teachings and initiations from the Pleiadians with Christine.

Transmissions of Light

Transmissions are energetic sessions channeled by the Pleiadians. Typically, the Transmission begins with a channeled dialogue from the Pleiadians. Each Transmission tends to work with a theme and brings a unique experience to every person in attendance. Each Transmission is completely different and brings what is most relevant to the moment and to the audience gathered.

These Transmissions create healing and energetic transformations, initiating you into a higher level of your light. They are highly transformational and allow you to take another step toward your Self. They work by transmitting healing light out to groups of people, so that everyone within the area receives these energies of light.

These Transmissions of Light open up initiations for you—initiations of your Higher Self through your cells. This can create healing through the physical body and the emotional body, and create new levels of spiritual awakening for each individual.

Transmissions are held in venues throughout the world and are open to the general public.

Three-Day Pleiadian Seminars

The Pleiadians channel a series of initiations over a three-day period specifically designed for these times. These initiations include activations and alignments into Higher Realm aspects of Self with the Pleiadians, the Lemurians, and all Galactic energies. There is work done within the crystal vortex in alignment with the Communication Portals in which you receive a series of awakenings for a rapid transformation of Self. The cells of your body go through a metamorphoses process; there is a rejuvenation process as a natural part of your birthright.

These events bring you in direct contact with the Pleiadians, forming a personal relationship with them. Over the three days you are moved into a deeper communication with the Pleiadians, the Lemurians, and all Galactic energies, as well as the Spiritual Realms. There are also strong alliances made with Mother Mary, and the Christ energy brings a strong self-resurrection energy to the seminars.

You are given step-by-step processes and practical tools with which you can navigate more steadily in your day-to-day lives. All energies from the Spiritual Realms are able to come and assist in these events because of the series of dimensional energies that are anchored, creating an energetic womb within the room that you are held in as you birth. It allows the Angels, Light Beings, and Masters to come into the workspace and assist you in your transformations.

There is a place held for each one of you who choose to come to this Seminar for your next step.

Online Classes

These online video classes are channeled by the Pleiadians; these classes will be from 30 to 60 minutes. There are many different series of classes available for you to choose for your transformation. Check them out online in the store.

These classes are profound, designed to bring you on a sacred journey of initiation.

Each online video class will bring to you:

🌱 The latest transformational energies from the Pleiadians' teachings.

🌱 Powerful initiations for realigning to your Higher Self.

🌱 Sets of tools for to work with in your day-to-day life.

For more information about all classes visit my Website at *www.christinedayonline.com*

Blog Talk Radio

Join me on the first and third Monday of each month on my radio show at 2:30 p.m. CST, for enlightening information and Transmissions from the Pleiadians. As we move deeper into the transition that is taking place on planet Earth, the Pleiadians tell us that the time has come to start mastering the energetic tools that will enable us to consciously complete our awakening and self-healing process.

Shows are available to listen to live or download from the Archives at *www.blogtalkradio.com/christinedayonline*

Free Pleiadian Broadcasts

The Pleiadian Broadcasts are available at regular intervals throughout the year on my Website (*www.christinedayonline.com*). The Broadcasts are typically aired six times a year. This format offers a unique opportunity to share with you the land in Grand Marais, Minnesota, and the ongoing work with the Communication Portals and the Stargate.

Come and receive the latest updates and teachings from the Pleiadians and the Galactic Community. Experience a powerful Transmission of

Light channeled from the Pleiadians. These are always an amazing part of our show. The Broadcasts are made available as the energies are ready to be released to humanity. All the Broadcasts are free for you to download, enabling you to be able to continue to work with the teachings.

Newsletters

Each month I send out a newsletter with a message from the Pleiadians and my personal message. This brings the latest updates of what is happening, what I am doing, and what the Pleiadians are making available for you. Visit my Website (*www.christinedayonline.com*) to sign up!

About the Work

I want to share and describe to you the two bodies of work that were channeled to me so long ago. They continue to be offered in many areas of the world and continue to unfold as extraordinary avenues for healing and awakening:

Amanae was the first channeled work that I anchored into the world. Amanae is a hands-on, multidimensional bodywork process that opens up the emotionally held blocks in the body. Amanae opens up a direct access for you to connect to your issues that are held in your physical body. As you consciously feel into an area, the emotion can leave your body, and healing can take place. This moves the body into a depth of healing on many levels, within the physical and emotional bodies. There is a deep spiritual transformation that takes place as the emotion moves out, and the light of the Self anchors into your cells.

Frequencies of Brilliance was channeled through me, and birthed at the exact same moment as Amanae. I have been initiating practitioners and teachers in this work since early 1999, and it has been my main work on the earth plane up to this time. This work continues to bring an enormous healing potential for clients. There are medical studies soon to be released documenting the impact this work has on a physical level as well as on the overall well-being of the client. These bodies of work are often referenced for bringing about miraculous healing. The truth is that these works, sourcing from the fourth, fifth, or higher dimensional realms, create self-healing as a natural part of the light of Self.

INDEX